MARCO POLO

C000179688

ZAK
YNT
HOS

KEFALONIÁ
ITHACA LÉFKAS

FREE!

THE TOURING APP

shows you the way...
including routes and offline maps!

GET MORE OUT OF YOUR MARCO POLO GUIDE

IT'S AS SIMPLE AS THIS

1 go.marco-polo.com/zak

2 download and discover

GO!

WORKS OFFLINE!

SYMBOLS

  INSIDER TIP   Insider Tip

 ★   Highlight

 ●●●●   Best of...

 ☆   Scenic view

🌐 Responsible travel: fair trade principles and the environment respected

PRICE CATEGORIES HOTELS

Expensive	under 100 euros
Moderate	60–100 euros
Budget	under 60 euros

Prices are for two people in a double room including breakfast in peak season

PRICE CATEGORIES RESTAURANTS

Expensive	over 20 euros
Moderate	15–20 euros
Budget	under 15 euros

Prices are for a meat dish with side dishes, a salad and a glass of wine from the barrel

CONTENTS

DID YOU KNOW?
Timeline → p. 14
Water flowing inland → p. 43
For bookworms & film buffs → p. 61
More than 1000 nests → p. 70
National holidays → p. 109
Budgeting → p. 115
Weather on Zákynthos → p. 116
Currency converter → p. 118

MAPS IN THE GUIDEBOOK
(124 A1) Page numbers and coordinates refer to the road atlas
(0) Site/address located off the map.
Coordinates are also given for places that are not marked on the road atlas
Maps of Léfkas Town and Zákynthos town, Argostóli and Olympia can be f[o]ound inside the back cover

(𝄞 A–B 2–3) refers to the removable pull-out map

INSIDE FRONT COVER:
The best Highlights

INSIDE BACK COVER:
Maps of Léfkada Town and Zákynthos Town, Argostóli and Olympia

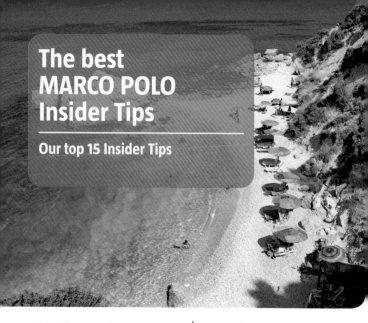

The best MARCO POLO Insider Tips

Our top 15 Insider Tips

INSIDER TIP Wines and more

The rural *Divino winery* on Kefaloniá not only has excellent wines but also produces aromatic rose oil vinegar → p. 41

INSIDER TIP Guided hikes

If you enjoy nature, want to know more about Mediterranean plants and hear all about Odysseus, then take a guided hike across Ithaca with *Ester van Zuylen* → p. 37

INSIDER TIP In a sea of flowers

On the terrace of the *Kástro* taverna on Kefaloniá you can sit below the Venetian castle between countless colourful flowers and enjoy great food at very reasonable prices (photo right) → p. 47

INSIDER TIP Eco-sightseeing

Enjoy a close and gentle encounter with loggerhead sea turtles by kayak in the *Marine National Park* of Zákynthos from July until September → p. 91

INSIDER TIP Special restaurant

As one of the most unusual restaurants in the Ionian Sea, the *Portokáli* on Zákynthos serves outlandish dishes with special colour harmonies and modern art, and sometimes even with live music → p. 76

INSIDER TIP Skin deep

Bathing in the sulphur springs at the small tiny cove of *Xigiá Beach* on Zákynthos will leave your skin feeling softer. After your swim, drinks can be transported down to the beach in a small wicker basket. For a relaxing and more gentle complexion (photo above) → p. 78

INSIDER TIP Dream accommodation

The name says it all: the small establishment of *Dreams* on Kefaloniá offers lovely accommodation in one of eight studios with green lawns that stretch all the way down to the beach and its private beach bar → p. 50

INSIDER TIP Alternative hotspot

Zákynthos has its fair share of free-thinkers and the popular meeting place for the alternative scene is the tiny café *34,* named after its house number. A delightfully messy, laid-back and affordable café attracting a politically-left and cosmopolitan crowd → p. 79

INSIDER TIP Under your own steam

One rather unique way to explore the Ionian waters is on a guided trip offered by a sporty couple on Kefaloniá. Not only do they rent out kayaks at *Seakayaking Kefaloniá,* but they also offer multi-day trips around Kefaloniá with visits to the small neighbouring islands → p. 103

INSIDER TIP Miniature golf in Stonehenge?

On Zákynthos you can forget the boredom of many miniature golf parks and go on a world trip – a themed course has scenes from all over the world such as the Golden Gate Bridge and Stonehenge → p. 78

INSIDER TIP A fisherman as host

In the taverna *Pórto Roúlis* in Drossía on Zákynthos, the ambiance is that of the oldtimes → p. 76

INSIDER TIP Clear view

You can see almost the whole island from *Áno Gerakári* on Zákynthos and you are far from any traffic – a beautiful place for a picnic → p. 67

INSIDER TIP Farmer with a forest taverna

In the *Oásis* on Léfkas, the hosts usually only serve products from their own farm: lamb and kid, cheese and yogurt → p. 58

INSIDER TIP Sleep surrounded by blossoms

Trífilli guesthouse on Kefaloniá is completely covered with flowering plants → p. 51

INSIDER TIP A rare tipple

If you like grappa, try the Zakynthian version in *Zépos* distilled by the restaurant owner's father → p. 77

BEST OF...

GREAT PLACES FOR FREE
Discover new places and save money

● *Discover nature*

In the botanical garden *Cephalonia Botanica* on Kefaloniá you will find yourself alone with the flora of the Ionian Islands, because apart from a few school groups, no one else visits. Information panels have the names of the flowers, herbs, trees and shrubs and you can also find a nice spot for a picnic. Entrance is free (photo) → **p. 42**

● *Be a knight*

The admission-free *Kástro*, above the Livátho Valley on Kefaloniá, looks like a medieval adventure playground for the whole family and offers a fantastic view over the fertile stretch of land to the sea and to the island mountains of Énos → **p. 43**

● *Noble living*

In the *Lixoúri Museum* you can experience how the rich Kefalonians lived more than a century ago, at no cost. The stately villa's ceiling frescoes alone would be unaffordable today → **p. 45**

● *Collect some Grecian pitch*

At the *tar springs in Kerí* on Zákynthos visitors can collect a small amount of pitch as it comes out of the ground and take it home as a free souvenir. Best to keep it in a very tight container ... → **p. 69**

● *Flamingo safari*

If you happen to visit the *Santa Maura* fortress between autumn and spring, you will spot hundreds of flamingos grazing in the surrounding flat wetlands – usually standing on one leg. A free bird-spotting site, perfect for photographing this elegant species → **p. 57**

● *Liquid gold*

During the winter you can see how olive oil is made at a modern *olive press* in Lithákia on Zákynthos (or hear the explanation throughout the whole year), a tasting is part of the experience → **p. 71**

( ) ( ) ( ) ( ) Dots in guidebook refer to "Best of..." tips

● *Regional cuisine*

To unveil the mysteries of Ionian Island cuisine, book an evening cooking course with Vassilikí and Giórgos Balí in the village of *Karavádos* on Kefaloniá. Herbs and other ingredients are gathered from their garden and then enjoyed with other international guests → p. 103

● *Ionian wine*

Wine has been cultivated on all the Ionian Islands for millennia. The white Robóla, which is considered to be typical of the islands, is mainly produced by the *wine cellars* on Kefaloniá. They are open to visitors and also offer free wine tastings → p. 43

● *Unique icons*

Icons are omnipresent in Greece but the Ionian Islands have evolved a distinct form of icon painting developed under the Venetian influence. In the *Zákynthos Museum* (photo) in the island's capital you can see classic Byzantine icons as well as works in the Ionian School typical of the islands. Most of these works are untitled which means, in a strictly theological sense, they are regarded as paintings rather than icons and are more Italian than Orthodox in style due to their Renaissance influences → p. 74

● *Hoping for miracles*

The saints play an important role in the life of the islanders, who pray to them for help. The *Church of Saint Dioníssios* in Zákynthos Town is very impressive and pilgrims visit the sarcophagus of the island saint all day long → p. 74

● *Listen to kantádes*

The Zakynthians have a reputation as the Greeks who love to sing. Everyone sings along when the typical Zakynthian *kantádes* are sung, as it happens every evening in the *Varkaróla Taverna* → p. 79

● *A private museum*

Many Greeks dream of owning their own museum. One man who has made this dream come true now runs the *Párko Eliés,* a tiny, bizarre outdoor museum in a former quarry located to the north of Zákynthos → p. 72

ONLY ON

BEST OF...

● **Simply dive in**
The rain plays no role when you are under water. In Limní Kerioú on Zákynthos you can book a short introductory dive course at both local *diving schools* → p. 101

● **Explore the underworld**
In the *Drongaráti Cave* (photo) on Kefaloniá, it may constantly be dripping from the ceiling, but nobody gets wet. Over the millennia the water has formed bizarre stalagmites and stalactites → p. 42

● **Ancient play things**
Playing with dolls is not a recent childhood pastime – proof of which is provided by the pre-Christian terracotta toys on display in the *Archaeological Museum* in Léfkas. Whether the ancient instruments were played to send the little ones to sleep is not known however → p. 54

● **Piety and pomp**
In the *Monastery of Saint Gerássimos* on Kefaloniá you can spend a dry hour when you descend into in the former hermitage of the pious man in the old monastery church and thereafter marvel at the precious interior of the new monastery church → p. 43

● **Make pottery turtles**
It could be a blessing in disguise if it rains on a Tuesday or Saturday. On these days the studio of the ceramicist *Hanne Mi* on Zákynthos is open to the public and you can try to make your own ceramic sea turtle – without having to register first → p. 77

● **Cloud landscapes**
Rain showers often produce bizarre cloud formations. One great place to watch the skies is at the *Fioro tou Levante taverna* in Áno Gerakári. Here, the whole of Zákynthos lies at your feet → p. 75

RAIN

RELAX AND CHILL OUT
Take it easy and spoil yourself

● *A day cruise to three beaches*
While you bask in the sun on the deck, the captain steers the boat from Nidrí to the three most beautiful beaches of Léfkas, past steep cliffs and maybe even dolphins → **p. 57**

● *Like Robinson Crusoe*
At the *Vatsa Club* on Kefaloniá you will feel as if you have been whisked away to a more peaceful world. On the beach next to the river mouth time seems to stand still, the relaxed mood of the regular guests and hosts add to the attractiveness of the hideaway, where you can also spend the night in your own small house → **p. 51**

● *Relax on the beach*
At Kefalonia's wide, sandy *Mírtos Beach,* there is nothing (not even water sports) to distract you from its main attraction: the sea. The beach has one solitary beach bar and is surrounded by steep, rocky cliffs which have been carved away by the waves since time began → **p. 49**

● *Exclusive treatment for the mind and body*
For 300 euros, you can spend five hours relaxing in the public spa at the luxurious hideaway *Emelisse Art Hotel* on Kefaloniá. The treatments can be booked separately and include Indian, Balinese or Tahitian → **p. 103**

● *No-moan zone*
While the kids spend time feeding the ducks, playing in hammocks and swinging under the trees or splashing around in water, parents can relax with a coffee at the small *Karavómilos* lake on Kefaloniá – there is something to please everyone here → **p. 106**

● *Horse-drawn carriage*
Experience the spruced up little town Zákynthos like it was in the old days with a trip in a *horse-drawn carriage*. The best time for this is in the early evening, when the lanterns bathe the old facades in a warm glow (photo) → **p. 107**

INTRODUCTION

DISCOVER THE IONIAN ISLANDS!

Boats that sail right into blue grottos, secluded coves where the iridescent Ionian Sea shimmers in every conceivable shade of green, turquoise and blue. White cliffs that plunge almost vertically into the sea and *olive groves* that sweep right to the coast. Picturesque villages, ancient castles, bathing beaches: Zákynthos and its neighbouring islands seem to have been made for holidays. Beautiful towns invite you to stroll and winding roads take you on island expeditions. Two *national parks* await exploration, old monasteries sit languidly and wine estates invite you for tastings – and the sun shines almost every day during summer.

Off the west coast of Greece, between the south of Albania and the north-west of the Peloponnese, lies a 240 km/149 mile *chain of twelve inhabited islands*. Othoní, north of Corfu, is closest to Italy and Zákynthos forms the southern end of the chain. Léfkas is only a few kilometres from the Greek mainland and there many small islands off its east coast while Ithaca nestles to the north of Kefaloniá. The straits, with green shores and mountains, are reminiscent of the lovely northern Italian lakes. The islands mostly have impressive cliffs that drop off into the sea which forms fine sandy beaches on Léfkas, Kefaloniá and Zákynthos. The interior of the

In the unspoilt island interior sheep still have the right of way – such as here on Kefaloniá

island is characterised by impressive landscapes of *rugged mountain ranges*, among the highest on the Greek archipelago.

Unlike many of the Aegean Islands, the Ionian Islands are relatively green. Large areas are covered with ancient olive woods and groves that are dotted with dark, slender cypress trees punctuating the forest of silver leaves that shimmer in the sun and lending the hilly landscape a flair of relaxed serenity. In some places dense *pine forests* can be found – and way up at Énos on Kefaloniá there is even a pine forest which has been declared a national park. Little wonder then that the diversity of the landscape attracts those who enjoy the outdoors and hikes. Some visitors want to explore the surprising world that lies beyond the island beaches such as the beautiful stalactite caves on Kefaloniá, the numerous *sea caves and grottos* on

1400 BC
The islands are settled by Greeks for the first time: Traces of a 50,000 year old settlement of Mycenaeans have been found

734 BC
Founding of a Corinthian colony on Corfu

229 BC
Corfu becomes the first Greek town under Rome's rule

395–1204
Byzantine period – the Ionian Islands are ruled by Constantinople. In the 12th century it is raided by the Normans; Zákynthos and Kefaloniá are part of the Kingdom of Sicily for 100 years

Zákynthos. Naturally most holidaymakers come to enjoy the beajches and the pleasantly warm sea. There are endless stretches of beaches with the finest sand, such as along the Bay of Laganás on Zákynthos or on Kefaloniá's Palíki Peninsula, but there are also sand and pebble beaches where there are crashing waves during rough seas. Many beaches are surrounded by pine forests or olive groves. But not only beachgoers get their money's worth –sailors, surfers, divers and water sports fans will all find their *favourite beach* on any of the islands.

Corfu (for more detailed information see the Marco Polo "Corfu" guide) is the most populous and economically the strongest of the Ionian Islands (pop. 103,000) but it is not the only one that is well developed for tourism. During the summer Léfkas and Zákynthos are also filled with more tourists than locals. On Kefaloniá and Ithaca however, tourism plays second fiddle. On both islands *agriculture* plays the more important role and on Kefaloniá, Léfkas and Zákynthos there is also the cultivation of vines and olives. Although there are fishermen everywhere, they cannot even meet the needs of the locals with their catch.

> **White sandy beaches stretching along imposing cliffs**

There are no archaeological excavations of national importance – due to their remote location the Ionian Islands were not an important area during antiquity. In the Middle Ages they (along with the rest of Greece) formed part of Byzantium, and

1204
The Venetians make the participants of the Fourth Crusade conquer Constantinople. The Ionian Islands are divided among Italian aristocratic families

1386
The Venetians take Corfu, in 1482 Zákynthos, in 1500 Kefaloniá and in 1503 Ithaca. Léfkas falls under Turkish rule in 1467 and is only taken under Venetian rule in 1684

1815–64
The Ionian Islands become an independent republic; albeit a protectorate of the United Kingdom

1864
Unification with Greece

thereafter to Venice. They have the *Venetians* to thank for the fact that the Ionian Islands – except for Léfkas which is closer to the mainland – were never under Turkish rule, unlike the rest of Greece which was under Ottoman rule for more than 450 years. As a result there are no Turkish-Oriental influences, no mosques or minarets. Instead of wooden bay windows, Venetian influenced *arcades* and multi storey houses are typical elements of the Ionian architecture. The folk music lacks the distinctive Aegean sound – and even in the visual arts the Ionian Islands have gone their own way. While the rest of Greece fell under the Ottoman rule in the 16th century (with the exception of the Venetian Crete) the *artists* on the Ionian Islands worked under the influence of Italy, they went to Italy to train and worked in Italian workshops. When Crete came under the Turkish rule during the 17th century, many Cretan artists moved to the Ionian Islands and their work then reflected Western influences: thus the artistic style of the *Ionian School* was born. The best overview of the school can be seen in the Zákynthos Museum.

A unique art style developed on the Ionian Islands

In addition to Venice, Britain also played a role in the fact that the Ionian Islands differ from the rest of the Greece. Napoleon conquered Venice in 1797 and during that same year he placed the islands under French rule. In the next few years, they were subjected to different rulers – France, Russia and England – until the Congress of Vienna in 1815 when they were declared a British protectorate as the „*Republic of Seven Islands*". The 49 years in which British Lord High Commissioners treated the islands more as a colony than a protectorate meant that the archipelago were provided with the a good *roas network* and modern *water supply* to the towns. Despite all the various foreign influences, the Ionian Islands remain a genuine piece of Greece. The islanders repeatedly revolted against foreign rule and supported the rest of Greece (despite a British ban) in their battle for freedom from the Turks in 1821–29. They pushed for the unification of their islands to free Greece and in 1864 Corfu and the other Ionian Islands were finally united with the motherland.

During the summer in the popular seaside resorts you will not find the typical Greek lifestyle anymore, there are lots of international influences. In August they are

1941–44
The Ionian Islands are invaded by Italian and German troops

1953
Severe earthquake

1967–74
Military dictatorship

Since 2010
Greece is kept from bankruptcy only through massive aid from the EU and the IMF

Jan/Feb 2014
Earthquakes damage over 1000 houses on Kefaloniá

2016
Greece is still reliant on financial aid

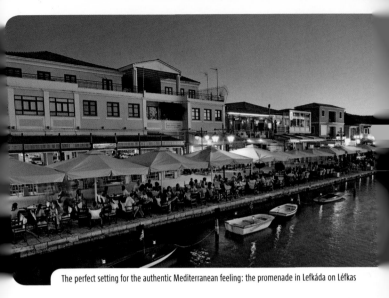

The perfect setting for the authentic Mediterranean feeling: the promenade in Lefkáda on Léfkas

dominated by the Italians and the rest of the summer months by the Dutch, British and Germans. However the towns have a *more traditional Greek character* – especially the villages in the island interior.

If you take a seat at a coffee house on the *platía* in a village then before long you will no longer be a stranger, most of the villagers pass the village square many times a day. Afterwards a stroll through the village will have a different feel to it, by then you will feel almost as if you belong there. The *coffee house* is the

> **Very soon you are no longer a stranger**

best place to meet the locals and to observe the rhythm of village life. One sees farmers who work the fields with donkeys or mules, children in school uniform, hear sthe travelling Roma promote their wares over the crackling speakers of their vans, old men having discussions and watches as they play *Távli* (a kind of backgammon), cards or checkers.

To get to know the Greece that is not yet dominated by tourism, you have to go for a walk through the olive groves and spend a leisurely hour in a *fishing port*. Then you may well be so taken by the real Greece that you might consider leaving your hotel and spending a night in a quiet mountain village.

WHAT'S HOT

1 Hot nights

Nightlife Zákynthos has a vibrant nightlife scene and the party hot spot is the main bar street in Laganás. Here the best DJs in the world spin their tracks in the *Rescue Beach Club (www.rescueclub.net) (photo)*, or they cool off after a night of dancing in the unisex shower of the *Cherry Bay Beach Club (www.facebook.com/groups/cherrybaybeachclub)*. Still looking for more? There is also the *Club Zero (www.facebook.com/Zeros ClubZante)* and the *Sizzle Club (www.facebook.com/sizzleclub. zante)* on the main road.

Volunteering **2**

In aid of a good cause ⊗ In the face of the financial crisis, the Greeks have pulled closer together. And because many young people are unemployed, social and nature conservation societies are finding it easier to recruit volunteers. The *Archelon* organisation *(www. archelon.gr)* on Zákynthos and Kefaloniá, dedicated to the protection of sea turtles and the animal rescue sanctuary *ARK* on Kefaloniá *(www.animalrescuekefalonia.com)* are two such charities to profit from these young volunteers.

In search of adventure

3 *Diving* The waters around Zákynthos are like an adventure playground. Caves, wrecks and night dives are popular among experienced divers. *Aquatic Efimia (Aquatic World | 1 Marinou Antipa | Agía Evfimía | Kefaloniá | www.aquatic.gr)* takes night dives to sunken ships. Night dives are also the speciality of the *Nautilus Diving Club (Vassilikí | www.underwater.gr)* where the search for fluorescent sea creatures gets going with underwater cameras. The *Diving Center Turtle Beach (Límni Kerioú) (photo)* makes motorcycle fans very happy.

There are lots of new things to discover on the Ionian islands. A few of the most interesting are listed below

Brave men

A visit to the barber UK hairdressers would delight at the experimental and daring hair styles paraded by Greek men – as female tourists on Zákynthos & Co already do. Modelling paste, beach-effect spray and texture powders belong to the essential tools of all good hair stylists on the Greek islands. One of the most popular hair trends is the undercut, buzzed short at the sides and long on top. While younger men sport the man bun, the more demure individuals prefer the good old ponytail. Only bald-headed men have less choice with the only option being the toupee. The prices will please everyone though: a cut at *G Coiffure (Odós Filíta 46)* in Zákynthos Town will set you back just 15 euros.

4

Steeped in history

Something old, something new Their glorious past and ancient traditions are sacred to the Greeks and are instilled into them from a young age at home and in school. However, young Greeks do not want to appear old-fashioned; their music is an eclectic mix of traditional instruments such as the bouzouki with pop and rock and traditional chords with metal sounds played by bands such as *Villagers of Ioannina City Zvara (www.face book.com/vic.epirus).* Traditional liquors such as black tentura with essences of cloves and cinnamon as well as mastika distilled from resin are the ingredients mixed into designer cocktails and mojitos. The beloved Greek flag also adorns fashionable sneakers *(www.celdes.com).*

5

IN A NUTSHELL

A GÍA, ÁGIOS

Travellers will see the words *Agía, Ágii* and *Ágios* everywhere. They are part of the names of villages and churches, fishing boats and car ferries. *Ágios* means saint, *Agía* is the female form and *Ágii* the plural of both. Blessed Virgin Mary has a special honorary name, *Panagía,* the Most Holy.

B EACH LIFE

In summer a dip in the sea is almost a daily occurrence for all the islanders. By the end of the summer the locals frequently quiz each other about how often did they go swimming. The quality of the beach does not necessarily play a big role, because most of them would prefer to sit in a taverna after their swim – or go to

one of the modern beach bars for a drink and snack served in lounge chairs. Lifeguards are only available on a few of the more popular beaches and then also only during high season.

Although sun loungers and umbrellas are rented out on many of the beaches, you can also just lie on your towel if you prefer. The deck chair rentals and taverna owners usually clean their beaches, and when money is available, so do the local municipalities. Private beaches have been allowed since 2014, but so far you hardly see any.

B YZANTIUM

The term Byzantium is hardly used anymore – it is the name given to an empire that existed for more than 1000 years

From Agía to Odysseus and beach life:
Discover the culture of the Ionian islands
in all its diversity

and many values and achievements of
the ancient world were kept alive well
into the late Middle Ages.

Byzantium was conquered by the Turks in
1453 and renamed Istanbul. Greeks from
Megará near Athens founded the city of
Byzantium around 660 BC; Emperor
Constantine made it the capital of the
empire in AD 330. When Emperor
Theodosius divided the empire in AD 395,
the city became Constantinople, the
centre of the Eastern Roman Empire.
While Rome and the Western Roman

Empire succumbed to attacks by Visigoths,
Vandals and Huns, the Byzantine Emperor
retained and expanded the empire. Under
Emperor Justinian I (AD 527–65) the empire extended to Italy, North Africa and
far into Asia Minor. The Ionian Islands
were still a part of the empire well into
the early 12th century.

EARTHQUAKES

Mild earthquakes are common on
the Ionian Islands. However, a cata-
strophic earthquake destroyed the south-

ern islands on the 9–12 August 1953. This destroyed 94 per cent of the homes on Zákynthos, 91 per cent on Kefaloniá and 70 per cent on Ithaca. That is why so few villages on these islands have any traditional architecture.

FAUNA

Cats and dogs are the animals that holidaymakers are most likely to encounter. Wild mammals have become rare. There are reportedly still rabbits, foxes, martens, hedgehogs and weasels. The bird life is richer and one can see magpies and golden orioles, hoopoes and jays, cuckoos, swallows and the Little Owl. In the more isolated mountain regions you can also still see buzzards and hawks, and herons along the flat coastal regions.

You may occasionally encounter a snake on hikes. The only one that is venomous is the sand viper; the non-venomous ones include the whip snake and Montpellier snake. Tortoises are common, scorpions rare. The sea has been exploited by over fishing and dynamite fishing, raising the price of fish. Dolphins are occasionally seen, there has never been a shark encounter in these waters.

FINANCIAL CRISIS

The crisis that became apparent in 2010 is far more than just an economic and financial crisis. It has touched every aspect of Greek society and forced changes in all reaches of life. Many taxes have been increased while wages, pensions and social benefits have been reduced. Many of the population are now impoverished and the social network inadequate.

It may take many years for Greece to recover. The islands are especially dependant on tourism; the islanders are very aware of this and will therefore do everything to ensure that the tourists enjoy their holiday.

FLORA

Olive trees and cypresses are the most distinctive trees of the Ionian Islands. Along rivers there are mighty plane trees; eucalyptus is the popular tree along avenues, and the sandy sea shores are home to the robust tamarisk. Large uncultivated areas are occupied by the *phrygana*, a mixed vegetation of broom, sage, butterfly lavender, thyme, oregano and dwarf juniper.

The dark native Kefaloniá pine grows along the Énos massif. In addition to the well-known fruit varieties, medlars are also grown in gardens; grapes thrive everywhere, in particular on Zákynthos and Kefaloniá.

HUNTING

Many Greek men are passionate hunters. According to one estimate by the Greek animal welfare society almost 400,000 men go hunting annually, many of them illegally. Hunting protection laws are in place, but are rarely observed. Early each year, hunters from all over the country meet on Zákynthos. On this island alone there are 13,000 officially registered hunting rifles are, but in reality the number is closer to 30,000.

ICONS

In the Orthodox Church icons are the representations of saints and biblical events on panel paintings. They are found in all the churches, but also in private homes and in vehicles. Icons are quite different from the religious images in our churches. They are the "gates to heaven" and they bring the saints into the home, making them ever present. They enjoy a lot of respect and are kissed, decorated with precious metals, embroidered curtains, precious stones, rings and watches. Icons are considered as the consulates of heaven on earth and are treated as if they were the saints themselves.

K IOSKS
Kiosks or *períptero* (the Greek singular) are situated in every square and in the towns and villages at the larger intersections. They are usually open from early morning until late at night and sell everything that might be needed urgently: cigarettes and razor blades, toothbrushes and combs, chewing gum, mineral water, condoms and much more.

K OMBOLÓI
Elderly men in particular like to play with a *kombolói*, a chain similar to a rosary. However, it has no religious significance, but only serves as a way to pass the time. The Greeks probably modified theirs from the Turkish prayer beads; the Greek worry beads always have an uneven number usually 13 or 17.

L OTTERY TICKET SELLERS
Lottery ticket sellers are as much a part of the Greek street scene as Orthodox priests and kiosks. Two lottery types are available: scratch cards with the possibility of winning instantly and tickets for the state lottery, where the numbers are drawn on Mondays.

O DYSSEUS
Ithaca is regarded as the home of Odysseus, the hero of "The Odyssey", the famous 2700 year old epic which is attributed to the legendary poet and singer Homer. The epic involves Odysseus' (the King of Ithaca) participation in the Trojan War, which Homer described in his

Windmill of change on Kefaloniá

other epic "The Iliad". After the end of the war, the hero and his companions set sail for Ithaca. The journey home took ten years and Odysseus was the only one to survive.

First Odysseus sailed with his men to the Thracian town of Ismaros which they then plundered. They set sail again and were blown off course to the land of the lotus eaters where his companions enjoyed some lotus plants (which put them in a dream state) and Odysseus was then compelled to force them back on board. Things got worse when they landed on an island of Cyclopes; one of them, Polythemus, later devoured two of his men. Then they visited Aeolus a mortal who had control of the winds who gave Odysseus a bag in which he could capture all the adverse winds except for the wind that blew towards Ithaca. But when Ithaca was finally in sight, his curious companions opened the bag and the fleet was driven by a violent storm to the Laistrygonians. They destroyed all the ships save for that of Odysseus and devoured many of the Ithacans. Those remaining went with their king to the island of the sorceress Circe, who turned many of the men temporarily into swine.

Next they survived the alluring song of the sirens – Odysseus plugged wax in their ears and tied himself to the mast to avoid temptation – only to have the six-headed monster Scylla kill six of his men. Then on the island of Trinacria, Zeus killed his remaining companions after they ate the sacred cows of the sun god Helios. Odysseus sailed away alone and came to the nymph Calypso, who lovingly held him captive for seven years. After which she was ready to let him go. Odysseus left on a raft and a storm washed him ashore on Corfu. The rulers for the local Phaeacians gave him a boat with which he finally returned to his home after his ten year odyssey.

RENEWABLE ENERGY

Greece has wind and sun in abundance yet both are not used nearly enough for energy production. Solar panels are widely used to heat water in private households and hotels. Photovoltaic

systems for energy production, which was pioneered for Greece on Crete, are still nearly absent on the Ionian Islands.

The generation of electricity from wind power is slightly better. On Kefaloniá three wind parks already feed about 50 megawatt of electricity annually into the power grid. On the other island wind turbines – largely funded by the EU – also add to the reduction of the petroleum products in the mostly outdated island power plants.

RELIGION

Almost all Greeks are Greek Orthodox Christians and those in the countryside are particularly pious.

For tourists the churches and many small chapels draw attention, because they look so different. Many are built in the Byzantine style with a dome and a floor plan in a cruciform; others follow the

Watch as time goes by at the Monastery of Agrílion on Kefaloniá

Italianate style with hall-like churches and high free-standing bell towers. However, none have the statues, confessionals boxes or fonts that you find in Roman Catholic churches.

You will see Orthodox priests all over the Ionian Islands. They always wear long, dark robes, have full beards and a hat under which one or more long braids hang out. Orthodox priests are allowed to marry before their ordination. They are paid by the state.

Orthodox Church services often last two to three hours. Only a few worshippers hold out that long so there is a constant coming and going and people often even chat amongst themselves during the service. Its main feature is the antiphonal singing of the daily liturgy which is celebrated by priests and some laity. An important ritual in the Greek Church is the kissing of the icons.

Orthodox Christians do not recognise the Pope as the head of Christianity. The schism in the church came about in 1054, because the Orthodox believe that the Holy Spirit only emanated from the Father, while the "papists" believed that it also emanates from the Father and the Son.

WASTE DISPOSAL

The waste generated on the island has to be disposed of almost entirely on the island. There are no incinerators and the waste is either burned out in the open air or turned into the soil. Recycling is still in its infancy, because the further processing of separated materials must be done on the mainland, with the added cost of transport. This is also the main reason why there is still no refund system for bottles and cans in Greece.

FOOD & DRINK

Greek restaurants and tavernas are not a paradise for gourmets. You will search in vain here for gourmet restaurants such as those found in France and Italy. Yet while Greek cuisine has remained down to earth and unpretentious it is still nonetheless very tasty and this is because the Greeks value good, fresh regional ingredients.

The choice of restaurants and taverna on the island is huge. Many open at 9am and serve full English breakfasts and various *omelettes*.

The majority of Greek restaurants stay open continuously, serving guests from noon until midnight. For those just wanting a snack, there is a growing number of modern American style snack bars, but also numerous small

barbecue stalls and bakeries. Many of them sell different types of *píttes*, puff pastries with various fillings. *Spanakópitta*, filled with spinach, *tirópitta* with goat cheese, and the *loukanikópitta* with sausage. A sweet version from northern Greece is *bougátsa*, which is filled with a light *semolina pudding* and dusted with powdered sugar.

TAVERNAS

A taverna is a traditional eatery that is more informal than a modern Western restaurant. Real *tavernas* are always simply furnished with wood or metal tables, usually covered with plastic covers or plain tablecloths. To keep the

Dine like the Greeks: companionship, atmosphere and ambience are more important in Greece than sophisticated cuisine

tabletop clean, the waiter will cover it with a *piece of paper*. Once done, he will immediately return with a basket of bread – for which you must pay – some paper serviettes and some cheap *metal cutlery*. You will need to go through to the kitchen (or look on the hot plate) to see what is on offer or you can ask the waiter for his *recommendations*.

In restaurants the locals are hardly ever handed menus as they say nothing about the quality of the dishes but there

are written menus specially for foreigners. Everyone at the table orders several dishes and the waiter then brings them all to the table simultaneously. The Greeks do not follow a specific order or even a menu composition. Appetizers, salads and main dishes (whether hot or cold) are all placed on the table at the same time. If you want to avoid this, you should order every course separately. All the dishes are placed in the centre of the table so that everyone can help themselves. The wine is poured

békri mesé – a type of pork stew with peppers in a lightly spicy sauce

bourdéto – fish or meat (rarely) dish in a spicy tomato sauce with onion, garlic and red pepper. As appetizer mostly prepared with *galéo* (dogfish), as main dish with *skórpios* (scorpion fish) or *pastanáka* (stingray)

briám – ratatouille

chtapódi ksidáto – octopus pickled in vinegar and oil (photo left)

fasoláda – bean soup

jemistés – peppers stuffed with rice, minced meat, tomatoes and aubergines

jouvétsi – stew that is baked in a clay pot – beef with rice shaped pasta, topped with grilled cheese

karidópitta – walnut cake (photo right)

kléftiko – roast lamb or goat meat with potatoes

kreatópitta – meat baked in puff pastry

láchanodolmádes – small cabbage rolls with lemon egg sauce

loukanikópitta – spicy pork sausage in pita bread

márides – crispy fried sardines, eaten with skin and bones, head and tail

pastitsáda – pot roast in a tomato sauce served with noodles

patsária – beetroot salad

revithókeftédes – chickpea fritters, usually served with a yoghurt dip

rewáni – semolina cake

riganáda – toasted bread topped with feta, tomatoes, olives and oregano

savóro – marinated sardines with currants, served hot or cold

sofríto – veal slowly cooked in garlic, white wine sauce

stifádo – usually beef (sometimes rabbit) stew with vegetables in a tomato sauce flavoured with cinnamon

into small glasses, and everyone toasts each other with *"Stin ijía mas"* – to our health!

Authenic tavernas usually only serve fruit for dessert, and coffee is rarely available. The bill is issued for the entire table, however, in recent years tavernas have started to allow foreigners to pay for their meals separately. *Seafood* and fresh fish are often calculated according to weight, so the price on the menu is often the price per kilogram. In order to avoid any unpleasant surprises, it is best to be present while the produce is weighed so that you can immediately ask the price.

OUZERÍ AND KAFENÍON

Traditional Greek restaurants are also *ouzeríes* – a place for locals to drink small carafes of the *national drink oúzo*. *Oúzo* is an anise liquor served with small dishes of octopus, fish and meat dishes, snails, eggs, biscuits, bread, salads or simply just olives, cucumbers and tomatoes; in contrast to other eateries here you order a little bit of everything. You can also let the host decide and simply order *pikilía* and *mezédes* (mixed hors-d'œuvres).

Greek *coffee houses* are the meeting place of the local men. In the tourist centres they are found either between Western style bars and cafés or out in the suburbs, but in the villages the *kafeníon* is still the *centre of social life*. There is no obligation to eat or drink so you will often see full *kafenía*, where no one is drinking. The locals sit together and discuss God, the world and Greek politics, or play *Távli*, checkers or cards. If you order coffee you have to specify exactly how you want it. When Greek coffee is made, the water, the coffee and sugar are all boiled up together.

Kafé ellinikó comes in many variations: *skétto* (without sugar); *métrio* (with a little sugar); *glikó* (with lots of sugar) and *dipló* (a double). Instant coffee is generally ordered as *neskafé* – either *sestó* (hot) or *frappé* (cold) and it is always best say how sweet you want it. The younger Greeks especially drink *freddo capuccino* or *freddo espresso*, both of which are served in large glasses with lots of ice cubes. During the colder seasons or in the evening they also drink a *rakómelo*, warm raki sweetened with honey and spices.

Olives and ouzo: essential tastes for the authentic island experience

SHOPPING

The souvenir shops in the cities and seaside resorts often have mass produced wares, which are at best produced on the Greek mainland. It is a better option to buy from the island artisans themselves or to shop in the small shops of the agricultural cooperatives. The souvenir shops and the supermarkets in the resorts are usually open daily from 10am until 10pm/11pm during the summer months. In the cities, supermarkets and shops catering to locals are closed on Saturday afternoon and Sundays. Many retail outlets also close on one or two afternoons during the week and have a long afternoon break from 1.30pm to 5pm.

ALMONDS & CO

The Palíki Peninsula on Kefaloniá is famous for its almond specialities: *mándoles* (roasted) and *barboulé* (caramelised) almonds. No visitor leaves Zákynthos without *pastélli*, sweet sesame and honey bars, or *mandoláto*, a soft nougat variety The small currants of Zákynthos and Kefalonià are also delicious.

CERAMICS

Ceramics from all over Greece (including copies of ancient painted vases) are offered in many shops. The best ceramicist on the island is the Norwegian Hanne Mi (see p. 77), who also offers private ceramic courses in her studio/showroom on the Skopós Peninsula on Zákynthos.

FASHION

Greece has an exotic and diverse taste in shoe fashion. Greek women's fashion is on sale in several boutiques in Zákynthos Town.

JEWELLERY

There are numerous jewellery shops especially on Zákynthos. The jewellery is slightly cheaper than elsewhere in Europe. Be sure to always check the quality though! There is no guarantee that it is produced in Greece as most jewellers buy from wholesalers and trade fairs all over Europe. The most beautiful jewellery shop of all the islands is in Kióni on Ithaca (see p. 36).

Shopping along the roadside: honey, wine and olive oil – agricultural products are typical of the Ionian Islands

OLIVE OIL

The best Greek olive oil is available in all the island towns. However, due to airline regulations for the transport of liquids, you can only legally be able to take it with you if you buy it at the airport after passing through the security checkpoint.

OLIVE WOOD

Olive wood carvings, including plates, salad servers, bread boards and bowls, are quite rare on the Ionian islands nowadays and also relatively expensive, because the wood has to dry for ten years before it can be processed.

PERFUME

On Kefaloniá and Zákynthos small businesses make eau de toilette. The labels are not very fancy, but the scent is pleasant and not available outside of Greece.

TURTLES

Turtles in the form of plush toys, plastic animals, fridge magnets and in ceramics are available especially on Zákynthos. In contrast to real turtle shells, they may be taken home.

WINE AND SPIRITS

There is a good selection of Greek wines in the *Cáva* shops in the towns. On Zákynthos, Kefaloniá and Léfkas you can visit wineries and buy wine directly. Lefkáda has a shop that sells liqueurs, brandy and oúzo still produced by themselves, sometimes also straight from the barrel.

ITHACA

The island of the hero Odysseus, known locally as Thiáki (Ithaca to us), is off the eastern coast of Kefaloniá, from which it is separated only by a narrow inlet.

Ithaca (pop. 3200) is 24 km/15 miles long and 6 km/3.7 miles wide; the northern and southern parts of the island are connected by a 600 m/656 yd wide isthmus. When driving along the scenic roads of the island you will have fascinating views of bays and coastline. Most of the villages are located in the hilly, fertile northern part of the island. The villages are increasingly becoming depopulated as fewer young people are willing to accept the low wages and hard labour of the agriculture and fishing industries. Thus the main area of the island now lies in the south, in the island capital of *Vathí*, and the nearby mountain village of *Perachóri*.

It is certain that Ithaca was already populated during the times of the Trojan War around 1200 BC. Whether the island really had a king named Odysseus, is doubtful. The Ithacans themselves believe the myth – and they also try to encourage tourists in this belief. As a result there are numerous places on the island – springs, beaches, caves and plains – that are said to be linked to "The Odyssey". Often there will be signs explaining this connection. Even if these spots are just myths and legends and not historically real, the beautiful surroundings often make the walk there worth it.

Photo: Vathí harbour

Tourists are an unusual sight in the former Kingdom of Odysseus – tourism plays a minor role on Ithaca

SIGHTSEEING & PLACES

AETÓS (127 E3) (*∅ D9*)

The ancient city Alalkoméne was once situated on the slope of the 380 m/1246 ft mountain south-west of Vathí. It was settled from about 1400 BC to Roman times. On the summit there are some well preserved cisterns and a part of the wall of the Acropolis that dates from the 5th century BC. On the pass between the eastern and western coast, where the road that leads from Vathí to the ferry terminal and the overcrowded (during summer) Bay of Pisoaetós, one can still see several large hewn stones from a Hellenistic tower.

ANOGÍ ★ ☀ (127 E2) (*∅ D8*)

The small mountain village lies about 500 m/1640 ft high on a plateau strewn with bizarre boulders, some as large as 8 m/ 26 ft. On the main road is the church of the Assumption of the Virgin Mary with campanile and well preserved frescoes

The small lanes in Kióni are idyllic – and what Odysseus perhaps longed for on his epic journey...

dating back to 1670. *The key is in the kafeníon next door, open until approx. 1pm*

ARCHAEOLOGICAL MUSEUM
(127 F3) *(Ⓜ D9)*

On display are finds from Alalkoméne, on the slope of Mount Aetós, such as ceramic votives from the Doric sanctuary of Apollo built there. *Tue–Sun 8am–2.30pm | free admission | Vathí*

ARETHOÚSA SPRING ★ ☼
(127 F4) *(Ⓜ E10)*

A beautiful 90 minute hike leads from Vathí to the spring at the base of a steep rock face on the south-east coast of the island. It is here that Eumaeus, Odysseus' swineherd, brought his masters pigs to drink. From the port, follow the "Arethoúsa Spring" signposts through the town and then continue on the narrow asphalt road until you reach a sign where the narrow footpath down to the spring begins.

DEXIÁ BAY (127 E3) *(Ⓜ D9)*

Legend has it that the bay with the small pebble beach is the Homeric Bay of Forkinos, where Odysseus was dropped off by the Phaeacians from Corfu.

KIÓNI ★ (127 E1–2) *(Ⓜ D8)*

Kióni is regarded by many as the most beautiful place on the island. The village lies at the end of a bay surrounded by olive and cypress trees. Here you can rent motor boats and head out to some picturesque bays: on foot or by boat you can reach several small pebble beaches in just a few minutes. In summer ferries connect the neighbouring village of *Fríkes* to Léfkas.

MONASTERY OF KATHARÓN ☼
(127 E2) *(Ⓜ D9)*

The monastery lies at 556 m/1824 ft and its freestanding bell tower has the most amazing view over large parts of the island. *Mon–Fri 8am–8.30pm*

NAUTICAL AND FOLK MUSEUM
(127 F3) (*ⅢD9*)
Small local museum in a converted power station. Because Ithaca has been a seafaring island since the time of Odysseus, many of the displays reference the sea. *May–Oct Mon–Sat 9am–1pm, July/Aug also 6pm–10pm | admission 3 euros | Vathí*

GROTTO OF THE NYMPHS
(127 E3) (*ⅢD9*)
After his successful return to Ithaca, Odysseus left his belongings in the care of the nymphs – mythical creatures that lived in a small cave above Dexiá Bay. The ceiling caved in during an earthquake in 373 BC. *It is extremely dangerous to enter the cave; take a torch to illuminate the inside of the cave from the outside!*

PERACHÓRI ☆ (127 E3) (*ⅢD9*)
Only 2 km/1.2 mile above Vathí at an altitude of 300 m/1863 ft is the island's largest village (pop. 500). Between the houses on the slopes, there are terraced vineyards and olive groves; the view of the harbour bay is extraordinarily beautiful. Unfortunately there is a lack of appealing tavernas. Several ruins testify to a medieval settlement in the area. Right at the lower village entrance, on the left side of the road, are the remains of a Venetian house and a church, where the remains of some frescoes can still be seen. In the village centre a sign points the way through olive groves to the ruins of *St John's church* with some more frescoes.

STAVRÓS ★ (127 E2) (*ⅢD8*)
The largest village in the north of the island (pop. 350) is situated on a mountain ridge, with views of both the east and the west coast of Ithaca. On the village square there is a bust of Odysseus, a board explaining his odyssey home and a 1:50 replica model showing what Odysseus' palace could have looked like 3250 years ago. A cul-de-sac leads you down to the bay of *Pólis*. In the coastal plains traces of an ancient stadium have been found; on the mountain ridge on the other side of the bay, there are also the remains of some ancient walls.

VATHÍ (127 F3) (*ⅢD9*)
The island's capital (pop. 2000) is a tranquil town with no significant sights. It lies at the inner end of a long fjord-like bay, which winds its way to the sea. It can get quite lively at night in the cafés along the waterfront, which gives one the feeling of sitting on the shores of a large lake. There is a pre-1953 villa in the harbour designed by German architect Ernst Ziller; the majority of houses were destroyed by the 1953 earthquake, including the quarantine station dating back to the 19th century on the islet of *Lazaretto*. You

★ **Anogí**
Mountain village between bizarre boulders and a church decorated with frescoes → p. 33

★ **Arethoúsa Spring**
Hike through wild natural beauty to a legend → p. 34

★ **Kióni**
The most picturesque village of the island is virtually car-free → p. 34

★ **Stavrós**
Find out what Odysseus' palace once looked like → p. 35

MARCO POLO HIGHLIGHTS

can swim to the islet and excursion boats also make trips to the short gravel beaches on the other side of the bay.

FOOD & DRINK

INSIDER TIP **MÝLOI / MILLS**
(127 E2) (*D8*)

Situated right on the harbour front, this taverna is a feast for the eyes. Traditional recipes are given a creative twist. *Kióni | on the harbour | Moderate*

SIRÍNES (127 F3) (*D9*)
Great selection, very tasty roast pork. *Evenings only | Vathí | in the alley parallel to the waterfront promenade | www.sirines.eu | Expensive*

TRECHANTÍRI (127 F3) (*D9*)
Every morning, food is freshly cooked and baked in this traditional taverna and displayed in the counter for guests to select their particular dish in the evening. Outdoor seating is available on the main shopping street and locals like to come here at lunch time for the cheap vegeta-ble dishes. *Vathí | parallel alley to the coastal road near the post office | Budget*

SHOPPING

ELPINÓR (127 F3) (*D9*)
Authentic shop on the waterfront with ship pictures, bric-a-brac, painted pebbles and jewellery. *Vathí | Paralía 160*

INSIDER TIP **TECHNÍMA**
(127 E2) (*D8*)

Regarded as the best jewellers on all the islands, this studio is housed in a 500-year old stone building with a medieval wine press in the centre. Decorative Greek jewellery and accessories from 15 euros. *Kióni | on the harbour | www.tehnima.com*

SPORTS & BEACHES

INSIDER TIP **ÁGIOS IOÁNNIS BEACH**
(127 E2) (*D9*)

100 m/328 ft long, 15 m/50 ft wide isolated pebble beach without a taverna, sparsely visited, but with some good snorkelling.

FILIÁTRA BEACH (127 F3) (*E9*)
Really nice, child friendly pebble beach in front of old olive trees, however at the height of summer there is often loud music and people camping rough.

GIDÁKI BEACH (127 E3) (*D9*)
The most beautiful, sandy pebble beach approx. 6 km/3.7 miles northeast of Vathí is only accessible on foot or by boat. In midsummer a small beach bar also opens.

MOTORBOATS
Motorboats (up to 30 h.p.) can be hired in *Kióni* harbour (*Kioni Boat Hire | tel. 2674 03 11 44*) and Vathí (*mobile tel. 69 49 93 56 70 | rentaboatithaca.com*) without a boating license.

LOW BUDGET

Taverne Kalkánis in Vathí not only serves traditional taverna food but also pork or chicken gyros in pitta bread for just 2.60 euros to take away or eat at one of the tables provided.

There is no bus line running between the harbour and the town centre. The only option is to hitchhike – a completely safe way to travel around the islands. The best way is to ask a driver on the ferry before arrival.

INSIDER TIP HIKING

Four times per week from April to October (excluding August) Ester van Zuylen offers 3–4 hour guided hikes in groups of maximum 10 people from different starting points. *16–20 euros without transfers | Island Walks | www.islandwalks.com*

ENTERTAINMENT

Theatre performances and concerts are occasionally held in Vathí. The evening meeting place for the locals and Greek tourists is the crêperie *Mílos*, directly on the pier.

WHERE TO STAY

CAPTAIN YIANNIS (127 F3) (𝄐 D9)
This spacious facility, with 26 apartments and hotel rooms, is on a gentle slope on the east side of the Bay of Vathí, it stretches down to the waterfront where there is also a swimming pool and bar. All rooms are well-appointed and individually decorated. Very good value for money! *Vathí | tel. 26 74 03 33 11 | www.captainyiannis. com | Moderate*

MÉNTOR (127 F3) (𝄐 D9)
Housing 36 rooms and apartments, this is the island's largest hotel which has been fully modernised and refurbished. Situated in a stunning location on the innermost end of the bay, the hotel has a splendid breakfast terrace area. Make sure to book a room with a ⛵ sea view. *Vathí | tel. 26 74 03 24 33 | www.hotelmen tor.gr | Moderate*

NOSTÓS (127 E1) (𝄐 D8)
Two storied, well-maintained hotel with swimming pool, 900 m/2952 ft from the nearest pebble beach. *27 rooms | Fríkes | tel. 26 74 03 11 00 | www.hotelnostos-ithaki.gr | Expensive*

Chic and simple: the Perantzáda Hotel

PERANTZÁDA ... 1811 (127 F3) (𝄐 D9)
Boutique hotel with a villa dating from 1811 at its heart, decorated with furniture by renowned designers. *19 rooms | Vathí | tel. 26 74 03 34 96 | www.perantzadaho tel.com | Expensive*

INFORMATION

POLYCTOR TOURS (127 F3) (𝄐 D9)
Trip bookings, general information, also mountain bike rentals. *Platía Drakoúli | Vathí | tel. 26 74 03 31 20 | www.ithaki holidays.com*

FERRY CONNECTIONS

Year round connections between Pisoaétos and Sámi (Kefaloniá), Killíni/Peloponnese and Nidrí (Léfkas). *Information: harbour police Vathí | tel. 26 74 03 29 09 or Delas Tours | Vathí | tel. 26 74 03 21 04*

KEFALONIÁ

The spelling of its name is just as varied as the island itself. **Besides Kefaloniá, you will also see Kefallinia and Cephalonia. The diversity of Kefaloniá (pop. 36,000) is best experienced on a trip around the island. Set aside at least three days – after all the island does cover 303 square miles.**

In the north, it appears as if the Érissos Peninsula seems to cling to the coast of the neighbouring island of Ithaca. There are only two villages, *Ássos* and *Fiskárdo*, on the coast; the majority of the islanders live in mountain villages in the hinterland. The lower regions of the slopes are covered in olive and cypress tress while grain, fruit and vegetables are cultivated on small plateaus. On the bare slopes of the steep west coast of the *Érissos*

Peninsula, sheep and goats graze above the breathtakingly beautiful, winding scenic road.

The *Palíki Peninsula*, with *Lixoúri* as its most important town, is completely different. In the east it is bordered by the shallow, lagoon-like Bay of Argostóli and from there rises gently to the west coast which in turn falls steeply down to the Ionian Sea. Long, reddish sand beaches line the south coast with its low, white limestone cliffs, a few hotels and an almost desert-like hinterland with deep, dry stream valleys and mesa-like plateaus.

The island's core is a powerful central mountain range with the 1131 m/3710 ft high, mostly barren Agía Dínami and the fir-lined 1628 m/5340 ft high Énos.

Beautiful places, lots of beaches:
the largest island in the Ionian Sea
has many different aspects

Parallel to it, is the 1082 m/3549 ft high mountain range, the Kókkini Ráchi, on the east coast. In these mountainous regions there are very few settlements. That is why in the two harbour towns of *Argostóli* and *Sámi* came into being in the coastal plains with sheltered bays. *Livátho*, a low lying, particularly fertile region south of Argostóli, is also very densely populated.

As with everywhere else on the islands, the 1953 earthquake also caused serious damage on Kefaloniá. Towns and vil-lages had to be rebuilt anew, only in the north, on the Érissos Peninsula, the old character of Kefaloniá is still evident in its quiet villages.

During ancient times there were four independent town states on Kefaloniá. Ancient Pale and Pronnoi have disap-peared, there are a few insignificant ruins of ancient Krane near Argostóli but at Sámi there are still large parts of the mas-sive ancient city wall.

Kefaloniá is also popular with film buffs as "Captain Corelli's Mandolin" was shot

Bathing in the small wind-sheltered bay in Ássos

here in the summer of 2000. Directed by John Madden it stars Nicolas Cage, Penelope Cruz and John Hurt. It is set in the time of the Italian occupation of the island during the Second World War and the assassination of Italians by German soldiers in 1943.

SIGHTSEEING & PLACES

ARGOSTÓLI (128 B2) *(᠁ B11–12)*
MAP INSIDE BACK COVER

Founded in 1757 by the Venetians, the administrative capital (pop. 9000) of the island stretches along one side of the Bay of Argostóli, without a view of the open sea. The earthquake of 1953 left only a few old buildings standing giving the town a sober and modern feel. Argostóli is not your typical, picture-perfect Greek town and definitely not a place for bathing. The town attracts few tourists, unless a cruise ship just happens to dock at the town's modern cruise boat terminal. The business life mainly takes place on the 2 km/1.2 mile long waterfront promenade. There you will also find the bus station and the beautiful market with its attractive, large fruit and vegetable stalls. The venue for the evening *volta,* where half of the town seems to be out on a stroll, is the *Platía Valianoú* where children play outside until late in the evening and sometimes small concerts with Greek music are held on warm summer evenings.

In addition to the Korgialénios Library, the main tourist attraction is the INSIDER TIP *Ágios Spiridónis* church on the main shopping street, *Lithóstrato*. The inside was completely painted with Byzantine frescoes during the 1970s. The lower part of the left side wall is reserved for female saints, among them the Empress Theodora, who reintroduced the veneration of icons. She is fittingly represented with an icon in her hand. The upper part of the church represents biblical events, such as the Decent into Hell, the Healing of the Lame, the Nativity and Baptism of Christ. The most remarkable building in the town is the *causeway* that was erected over the shallow bay by the British in 1813. In 2016 it was transformed into a promenade. The locals like to fish from its walls. In its centre is an obelisk, which the Kefalonians dedicated to the British in thanks for the bridge.

ÁSSOS ★ (126 C3) (*M C9*)

The village of Ássos (pop. 100) lies at the inner end of a sheltered bay that is popular with yachtsmen. In the east it is bordered by terraced slopes and in the west by a headland with the remains of a 16th century *Venetian fortress (freely accessible during the day)*. It is connected to the main island by a narrow, rocky isthmus. The Venetians managed the north of the island from Ássos, the castle provided farmers protection from pirate raids. From the partially accessible castle walls there are great views, lush greenery has grown over remnants of the building inside. During a stroll through the village, the serious damage by the 1953 earthquake is evident, Ássos never fully recovered from the quake. Only a few elderly people live here in winter, but during the summer the short pebbly beach is very popular.

INSIDER TIP CAVA DIVINO
(128–129 C–D3) (*M C12*)

Founded in 1864, the island's most sophisticated winery is still housed in its original historic building. The winemaker personally shows visitors around his premises, inviting them to taste the wines which include a home-distilled retsína and robóla, an island speciality with an especially low acid content. They also produce special vinegar aromatised with traditionally extracted rose oil. *Open during the day | Pessáda, in the village centre*

MARCO POLO HIGHLIGHTS

CEPHALONIA BOTANICA ● (128 B2) (🗺 B12)

On the outskirts of Argostóli a small foundation maintains a small botanical garden with a babbling brook. Information

Fish in Fiskárdo – can there be a prettier setting for a meal?

panels list the indigenous plants in Greek and English and also give their scientific Latin names. *Mon–Fri 9am–2pm | free admission | on the southern outskirts of the town, signposts along the coastal road*

DROGARÁTI CAVE ● (127 D5) (🗺 C11)

The 44 m/144 ft deep stalactite cave is very effectively illuminated. The com-

poser Míkis Theodorákis once conducted a concert here and one can only imagine what the atmosphere must have been like. *Daily 9am–4pm | admission 5 euros | on the road from Argostóli to Sámi*

ÉNOS 🌿 (129 E3) (🗺 D12)

You can drive on a 15 km/9.3 miles paved road up to the summit area of the highest mountain in the Ionian Islands, the 8 square mile area has been turned into a national park. When the paved road ends there is a further 7.7 km/5 mile long dirt track. The conservation of this large pine forest is particularly important. There are several nice picnic spots along the side of the road and a 2 km/0.8 mile circular walk around the peak which starts at the antennas in the forest (altitude of 423 m/1388ft). The view is particularly interesting for those who have flown from Zákynthos to Kefaloniá as you can see both airports from up here. *Signposted turn-off on the Argostóli–Sámi road*

FISKÁRDO ★ (127 D1) (🗺 C8)

The most beautiful (and most expensive) village on the island is on the curving shoreline of a small bay opposite Ithaca, and it was spared by the 1953 earthquake. The old, well-kept houses along the quay are the ideal backdrop for the lively hustle and bustle on the short waterfront; elegant yachts and small ferry boats enliven the port. The small village was named after the Norman ruler Robert Guiscard, who died here on one of his raids against the Byzantine Empire in 1085. The *Norman church* (its ruins seem rather incongruent in this environment) on the peninsula north of the port bay was built in his honour. For bathing there is the shallow rocky area at the edge of the peninsula as well as two small pebble beaches on either side of the village that are only a ten minute walk away. The olive groves that line the coast offer some welcome shade.

KARAVÓMILOS
(127 D5) *(ɯ C–D11)*

The village was newly rebuilt after 1953 and a small lake has formed between the sea and the village. A unique mixture of fresh water and sea water, which is sucked into the swallow holes on the Lássi Peninsula, comes up from the lake's bed. The water flows along the extremely short channel into the Gulf of Sámi and a restored waterwheel at a former flour mill was once fed by the lake's water. The waterwheel now stands on the site of the *Karavómilos* taverna *(daily from 10am | Budget)*, where the speciality is rabbit. *On the road from Agía Evfímia to Sámi*

KÁSTRO ●
(128 C3) *(ɯ C12)*

The Livátho plain is dominated by the 320 m/1050 ft high mountain ridge where the island capital of Ágios Geórgios was until 1757. Today the remaining Venetian castle, the *Kástro,* with about 600 m/1970 ft of walls is surrounded by a quiet little village,

whose ☙ cafés and tavernas have wonderful views over the island from their terraces. *Castle May–Oct Tue–Sun 8.30am–3.30pm | free admission | to the left above the road from Argostóli to Skála*

MONASTERY OF ÁGIOS GERÁSSIMOS
★ ● (121 D2) *(ɯ C12)*

The most visited monastery on the island stands on the edge of the Ómalon plain 400 m/1312 ft above sea level surrounded by mountains. In this region, the famous Robóla wine is cultivated and pressed in the ● cellars of the wine cooperative near the monastery *(visit to the Robóla Cooperative Winery incl. wine tasting May–Oct daily 9am–8pm, Nov–March Mon–Fri 7am–3pm | participation is free | www.robola.gr)*.

Today, the views of the monastery are dominated by a monumental and lavishly decorated marble church and the kilometre-long straight avenue that leads up to it. The old monastery church is more pleasant and modest, and in front of it is a plane tree that was planted by the saint himself in the 16th century. One of the frescoes in the interior shows the deathbed of St Gerássimos, whose soul is represented as a swaddled infant already committed to Christ. The

WATER FLOWING INLAND

Why does seawater flow inland and why is it sucked into the swallow holes on the Lássi Peninsula? And where does it go? It remained a mystery for a long time but this natural phenomenon was used to power sea watermills up until 1953. Two of these watermills have been preserved, one of which is a popu-

lar music venue on the island. Austrian geologists had the clever idea of pouring green dye into the seawater at Argostóli. Several days later it appeared in the cave of Melissáni right over the other side of the island. The lake's amazing colours are now completely natural again.

bones of the saint rest in a coffin and can be kissed by pilgrims through two small openings. At certain times, a priest reads prayers that believers have written on small pieces of paper. A trapdoor in the church floor leads down a steep ladder down into a cave where the island's saint once lived for a time. *April–Oct daily 3.30am–1pm and 3.30pm–8pm, otherwise 4am–1pm and 3pm–7pm | access signposted along the Argostóli–Sámi road*

INSIDER TIP MILAPÍDIAS MONASTERY
(128 C3) *(ꭥ C12)*

Opposite the Venetian castle of Ágios Geórgios lies one of the most interesting of the island monasteries. The main church houses a relic, supposedly a part of the right foot of the Apostle Andrew. More important however are the icons and frescoes in the old monastery church. The building dates back to around 1600, the oldest fresco has been dated to the 13th century. *Museum and old church Mon–Sat 8am–2pm | admission 3 euros | south of the road from Argostóli to Skála*

KORGIALÉNIOS LIBRARY
(128 B2) *(ꭥ B12)*

The library is the foundation of a rich Kefalonian; the building was faithfully restored after the 1953 earthquake. On display in the basement are various icons, folk art objects, costumes, furniture, agricultural and domestic appliances as well as historical photos. *Mon–Sat 9am–3pm | admission 4 euros | Argostóli | Odós Ilía Zérvon*

KOURKOUMELÁTA
(128 C3) *(ꭥ C12)*

The quiet village is probably the most beautiful and well-kept in the entire district of Liváthos, which was particularly hard hit by the 1953 earthquake.

The majority of the inhabitants back then were sailors. A shipping family supported them after the catastrophe with generous donations, many attractive houses were built. Today the gardens and streets are still carefully maintained, making for a pleasant short stroll through the village which you can follow with a visit to the central village café of INSIDER TIP *Marína (Budget)*.

LÁSSI PENINSULA
(128 B2) *(ꭥ B11–12)*

The hilly peninsula, where the island's capital Argostóli is situated, can also be explored on foot. The north of the peninsula is densely forested. At the other end of the forest away from the town, a historic sea water mill has been carefully restored and is a good example for understanding how the principle of the water mill works. This water mill is situated on the premises of the trendy

Boat trip on the crystal clear waters of the shimmering lake in front of the Melissáni Cave

Thalassómilos lounge restaurant (*Moderate)*, which makes a point of playing only international music in the evenings, to the delight of some locals. The British built a small *round temple* in the Doric style on the headland, which served as a beacon at the harbour entrance. After the 1953 earthquake, it was rebuilt in a simplified manner. 800 m/875 yd further on a signposted road branches off the coastal road and leads 700 m/765 yd to the *Monumento Caduti*. The memorial commemorates the 9470 Italian soldiers, who after Italy's capitulation in September 1942 refused to surrender to German troops and were consequently killed.

LIXOÚRI (128 B1–2) (*ꕤ B11)*
The capital (pop. 3500) of the Palíki Peninsula was founded in 1534 and still exudes the kind of grace and gentility which most towns on the Ionian Islands

lost after the 1953 earthquake. The market centre spreads out around the bus station and the social centre is the *platía* on the coastal road. One of the villas in the upper part of the town today serves as a ● *museum and library (Tue–Fri 9am–1.30pm, Sat 9.30am–12.30pm | free admission)*. Some of the rooms have partially restored ceilings that were painted over 100 years ago, furniture from every period as well as some icons are also on display. *Frequent ferry service between Argostóli and Lixoúri around the clock*

MELISSÁNI CAVE ★
(127 D5) (*ꕤ C10)*
A visit to the stalactite cave is a unique experience especially after noon as the sunlight is perfect then and as as a good part of it is a small lake accessible by boat. The sun filters through an opening which is framed by green trees and the

Demolished by earthquake and rebuilt again: the 200-year old Monastery of Agrílion in Sámi

light makes the crystal clear water shimmer in hues of blue and green. In the back of the cave, the water laps a small islet which in Antiquity was the site of a Pan sanctuary. *Daily 9am–at least 4pm | admission 7 euros*

METAXÁTA (128 C3) (*∅ C12*)

Like most of the villages in the Livátho plain, Metaxáta was almost entirely rebuilt after the 1953 earthquake. It has some very attractive villas and gardens. Near the village numerous shaft and chamber tombs from the late Mycenaean era were uncovered. *The excavations are fenced in sparsely. Access: turn off from the road between Peratáta and Metaxáta just behind the signposted turnoff to the monastery of Ágios Milapídias onto an unmarked dirt track and after 250 m/273 yd you will reach the fenced excavations.*

PÓROS (129 F2) (*∅ E12*)

The small harbour village (pop. 900) slowly evolves into a tourism centre but it is still very serene and calm. About 500 m/547 yd above the village and 6 km/3.7 miles on foot is the oldest monastery on the island, *Moní tis Panagías tis Atroú.* The first written evidence of it dates back to 1264. Behind the modern building, where the monks now live, the ⚡ old monastery and chapels rise up in the magnificent mountain solitude with superb views of the coast and the Peloponnese. *Access: just short of a mile from the shore the road branches off after a ravine on the Póros–Argostóli road*

SÁMI (127 E5) (*∅ D11*)

Sámi (pop. 1100) stretches out at the foot of a mountain, where the ancient city walls are still plainly visible. In the town itself there are the 5 m/16 ft high brick walls of a preserved *Roman bath.*
To reach the ruins of the town of ★ *Ancient Sámi* follow the signposted road at the north-eastern edge of the village to the *Monastery of Agrílion* (rebuilt after the 1953 earthquake) where the road forks for

the second time, and a sign to the left leads to the monastery, you take the road to the right. The ancient city wall that runs along the hill is clearly visible. At the point named *Ágioi Fanentes* near a white chapel it almost touches the dirt road. Right next to it is the ruin of a medieval monastery church and an ancient watchtower. Its preserved walls of carefully hewn stone reach up to 5 m/16 ft. A few minutes' walk from here, in the woods below the white chapel, are the ruins of a medieval church *Ágios Nikólaos (open to the public)*. A long, narrow sandy beach stretches from Sámi almost to Karavómilos.

SKÁLA (129 F4) *(Ø E13)*

At the southern end of the small seaside resort (pop. 550) whose long sandy beach is mainly visited by British tourists are the well preserved foundations of a *Roman villa (Mon–Fri 8.30am–3.30pm | free admission)*. A protective roof shelters two well preserved floor mosaics. One depicts the sacrifice of three animals, and the other one a young man who symbolises envy.

TZANÁTA (129 F3) *(Ø E12)*

In the village centre, a brown signpost leads the way to a Mycenaean *Thólos tomb (Tue–Sun 8.30am–3pm | free admission | 400 m/437 yd right of the main road to Póros)* dating back to the time around 1350 BC. The burial chamber under the grave mound is open to the public.

FOOD & DRINK

BEVERÍNOS (128 B2) *(Ø B12)*

Extremely affordable, authentic mezedopolío where you can order snacks to accompany a glass of wine, ouzo or grappa-like schnapps. *Argostóli | Odós St. Metaxá 9 | Budget*

COZY (129 F4) *(Ø E13)*

"Creative Greek cuisine" promises this beachside taverna – and it does not disappoint. Oyster mushrooms with Greek Talagári cheese, octopus tentacles with fennel and orange as well as roasted pork stuffed with leeks and smoked cheese are just some of the delicious specialities. The island's traditional robóla wine is the perfect accompaniment. *Káto Katélios | northern end of the coastal promenade | Moderate*

INSIDER TIP KÁSTRO ☃ (128 C3) *(Ø C12)*

The taverna at the entrance to the Venetian castle is a shady idyll in a sea of flowers. The host Spíros and his wife Níki serve affordable lunches, delicious cakes and cocktails, always accompanied by Greek music. *During the day | Kástro | Budget*

KIANÍ AKTÍ (128 B2) *(Ø B12)*

Approx. 30 tables are laid out on a wooden platform right above the water at this traditional ouzerí. The owner shows off

LOW BUDGET

The grill restaurants dotted around the market squares serve good-quality and affordable food at lunchtime. Two gyros in pitta bread for a mere 5 euros are enough to satisfy any appetite.

If you live in a studio or apartment with a kitchen and a frying pan, you'll be able to enjoy some fresh fish at a good price. The fishermen sell their fish every morning directly from their boats, at the quay of Argostáli, 300 feet from the market towards the exit of the bay.

an appetising display of freshly caught mussels and sea urchins in front of the taverna and fish in the chill counter. Excellent service and prices are also relatively cheap for seafood. They also serve the Kefalonian *kreatópitta,* a type of beef stew rolled into a strudel. *Argostóli | coastal road, directly at the cruiseship terminal | tel. 26 71 02 66 80 | Expensive*

INSIDER TIP MOLFETAS 🌐
(128 C2) (𝄞 B11)

The restaurant and guesthouse (6 rooms) in a restored old house in at Argostóli are both stylishly decorated with antiques. The hostess Katerína prepares tea from herbs that she collects herself and an excellent chocolate mousse; the meat served is organic. *Farakl*á*ta | tel. 26 71 08 40 07 | www.georgemolfetas.com | Expensive*

INSIDER TIP O AGRAPÍDOS 🌿🌐
(129 F2) (𝄞 E12)

Very inexpensive taverna serving hearty Greek food, with a magnificent view. Wine from their own vineyard, home-made bread, vegetables from their own garden. *Póros | above the harbour on the road to Sk*á*la | Budget*

ROSIE'S KITCHEN BAR 🌐
(127 D3) (𝄞 C9)

Originally from Thessaloníki, Rosie has created a laid-back oasis in the mountains where the more sophisticated islanders come to dine throughout the year. Herbal tea from the French press (served until 4pm) and organic egg omelettes are the real favourites. *From 9am | Kari*á *| on the main road | Moderate*

SHOPPING

ROBÓLA (128 B2) (𝄞 B12)
The small shop, named after the famous grape, stocks all the wines from the local

cooperative at affordable prices. Decent wines are also sold on tap. *Argostóli | at the market*

VOSKOPOÚLA
(128 B2) (𝄞 B12)

In this transparent bakery you can watch typical Kefalonian sweets being produced. Especially worth trying is the paste made of dried quinces. *Argostóli | Odós Lithostr*á*to 41 (near the clock tower) | www.voskopoula.gr*

SPORTS & BEACHES

ANTÍSAMOS (127 E5) (𝄞 D10)
5 km/3 miles northeast of Sámi this half mile long pebble beach is best known for being the set of numerous scenes from "Captain Corelli's Mandolin". It is nearly undeveloped and surrounded by trees.

KAMÍNIA BEACH (129 F4) (𝄞 E13)
Miles of isolated, shallow beach in the extreme south of the island opposite Zákynthos. *Access signposted on the Sk*á*la–Ratzakl*í *road*

KATÉLIOS BEACH (129 F4) (𝄞 E13)
A beach for sunbathers who like a waterfront café or taverna to enjoy a refreshing drink in between. Also ideal for non-swimmers and young children as the water remains shallow (depth of 1 m/3 ft) until quite far out – almost as safe as the non-swimmers' part of the pool at home.

MAKRÍS GIÁLOS & PLATÍS GIÁLOS
(128 B2) (𝄞 B12)

Beautiful sandy beaches with tavernas, lots of water sport activities and sun lounger rentals. Very popular in summer. On the side of the Lássi Peninsula that faces away from Argostóli. *Hourly bus connections to nearby Argost*ó*li*

Mírtos Beach - the perfect destination not just for romantic couples and photographers

MÍRTOS BEACH ★ ● (126 C3) (*m C9*)

A stunning 1 km/0.6 mile long and 100 m/109 yd wide beach with sand and dazzling white pebbles and cobblestones. The shoreline has been shaped by its longshore drift and high breakers. A steep winding road leads down the coast to the unspoilt beach with just a small cantína and car park at the bottom.

PALÍKI PENINSULA ★
(128 A–B2) (*m A–B12*)

There are many quiet, isolated beaches on the Palíki Peninsula. Red sand stretches from the low, white cliff coast along the entire southern coast of the peninsula from Lepéda to Kounópetra. The clay from the 20 to 30 m/65 to 98 ft high cliffs is traditionally used by the Greeks for cosmetic facial masks. The 20 m/65 ft wide and 1 km/0.6 mile long *Xi Beach*, with its shallow sloping shore line and red sand along a low, light cliff, is particularly beautiful, as is the 12 m/40 ft wide crescent shaped *Vatsá Beach* with a small fishing harbour at a river mouth. On Xi

Beach, *Baywatch Watersports (mobile tel. 69 37 41 40 90)* offers kayaks, parasailing, jetskiing and wakeboarding.

PÓRTO HÉLI BEACH (128 C3) (*m B12*)

150 m/164 yd long and 30 m/32 yd wide fine sandy beach at Svoronáta. To the west of the beach is a beautiful cave which you can swim into. There are parasols, canoes and paddle boats for hire on the beach and a kiosk to buy refreshments.

ENTERTAINMENT

BASS CLUB (128 B2) (*m B12*)

The island's trendy dance club; every Friday at around 11pm it is modern "Greek Night" (guaranteed no folk music), Fri and Sat international dance music until at least 3.30am. *Argostóli | Odós R. Vergóti | www.bassclub.gr*

LIBRETTO ◎ (128 B2) (*m B12*)

The island's culture café with a sensationally beautiful tile floor and a multifaceted,

Water with no boundaries – the infinity pool at the Emelisse Art Hotel

ecological orientation. Often live music, from *rebetiko* to the grooviest band on the island, the Singapore Slings. *Daily from 9am | Argostóli | Platía Kambánas (at the clock tower)*

WHERE TO STAY

INSIDER TIP DREAMS (129 F4) *(฿ E13)*
A large lawn separates the eight studios (each for up to 4 people) from the beach and the beach bar, where you can also have breakfast. The proprietor Panayíis is also very proud of his cocktail recipes. Very good value for money, open all year round. *Katélios | Ágios Barbara Beach | tel. 26 71 08 14 16 | www.kefaloniadreams. com | Budget*

EMELISSE ART HOTEL (127 D1) *(฿ C8)*
Nested above a small bay with long pebbly beach, the island's most luxurious hotel is a haven of nature situated amidst acres of forest and gardens near the picturesque village of Fiskárdo. The rooms are designed with natural materials and earth tones with stylish lounge furniture in reception areas. The hotel has two pools and a summer cinema while the buildings' architecture is in keeping with the island's traditional style. Free bike hire is also available for guests. *65 rooms | Fiskárdo | tel. 26 74 04 12 00 | www. emelissehotel.com | Expensive*

GERÁNIA
(126 C3) *(฿ C9)*
A peaceful guesthouse situated in a large garden, 300 m/328 yd from the shore. Parking available. *12 rooms | Ássos | tel. 26 74 05 15 26 | www.pensiongerania.gr | Moderate*

IONIAN PLAZA
(128 B2) *(฿ B12)*
The island's best hotel offering great value for money. A private car park is situated at the back of the hotel. The best accommodation is on the top floor with two-bedroom family suites. *47 rooms | Argostóli | Platía Vallianoú | tel. 26 71 02 55 81 | www.ionianplaza.gr | Moderate*

KARAVÁDOS BEACH
(129 D3) *(𝄞 B12)*

Hotel with swimming pool in the country-side some 150 m/164 yd from the beach and 2 km/1.2 mile east of Karavádos. Old fashioned, but comfortably furnished rooms in five individual buildings with at most three storeys. *77 rooms | Karavádos | tel. 26 71 06 94 00 | www.kbhotel.gr | Budget*

LINÁRDOS ≈⁄≈
(126 C3) *(𝄞 C9)*

Three-storey guesthouse only metres from the sea, all the simply and tastefully decorated rooms offer stunning views of the Bay of Ássos and the peninsula with its castle. Great value for money. *11 rooms | Ássos | tel. 26 74 05 15 63 | www.linardos apartments.gr | Budget*

RÉGINA RENT ROOMS ≈⁄≈
(127 D1) *(𝄞 C8)*

Guesthouse next to the main car park 50 m/164 ft above the harbour, ten rooms all with sea views. *Fiskárdo | tel. 26 74 04 11 25 | Budget–Moderate*

INSIDERTIP TRÍFILLI ◉
(129 D3) *(𝄞 D12)*

A friendly guesthouse with excellent taverna, expertly run by two Greek brothers and German-Swiss lady. Situated just 200 m/218 yd from the beach, the house is adorned with hanging flowers. The eco-logically-minded proprietors provide information and tips for walks and activities in the region. They also cook vegan and gluten-free dishes for their B&B guests if booked in advance. *Lourdáta | tel. 26 71 03 11 14 | www.trifilli.com | Budget*

INSIDERTIP VATSA CLUB ●
(128 A2) *(𝄞 A12)*

A hidden paradise right at the very end of the peninsula, the club overlooks the sea at a river mouth. There is a quaint beach taverna and six two-storey chalets, each with two modern furnished double rooms and a kitchen. You will not need anything other than your swimsuit here. *Ágios Nikólaos | mobile tel. 69 77 63 10 53 | www.vatsa.gr | Moderate–Expensive*

WHITE ROCKS ◉
(128 B3) *(𝄞 B12)*

The main house and garden bungalows are spread over 14 acres of old pine forest right on the sea. The beach is only access-ible from the water and from the hotel grounds. The entire facility was modern-ised a few years ago and was upgraded to be environmentally and energy-friendly. *163 rooms | Platís Giálos | tel. 26 71 02 83 33 | www.whiterocks.gr | Expensive*

INFORMATION

TOURISM BOARD (128 B2) *(𝄞 B12)*
Argostóli | coastal road, inside the cruise-ship terminal | tel. 26 71 02 22 48

FERRY CONNECTIONS

All year round, several times a day from Sámi to Pisoaétos (Ithaca) and Ástakos (mainland). All year round from Póros to Killíni/Peloponnes. All year round from Fiskárdo to the island of Léfkas (until 2018 to Nidrí, when the new port at Vassilikí opens, from there to Fríkes/Ithaca). From May to October twice daily between Pessáda in the south of the island and Skinári (Zákynthos).

FLIGHT CONNECTIONS

All year round two to three times a week with Sky Express to Zákynthos and Préveza (for Léfkas).

LÉFKAS

Léfkas, often called Lefkáda in Greece, is the only one of the Ionian Islands that is connected to the mainland by a bridge. And it is proof of the Greek art of improvisation: instead of building an expensive new one, they converted a matching sized ferry and berthed it sideways in the 50 m/164 ft wide canal that has made Léfkas (pop. 24,000) an island since Roman times. If a ship needs to pass, the "bridge" simply swings aside.

Just behind this original bridge at the north-eastern tip of the island, the road splits in two. One leads over a dam that was built by the British, to the capital *Lefkáda*. The other circles around the lagoon in the north and also passes along a half mile sandy beach with dunes and ideal conditions for windsurfers.

The coastal villages are almost exclusively on the eastern side of the island. In almost every one of them one has the impression that one is standing on the shore of a lake that is surrounded by mountains and hills. In the north only a narrow sound separates Léfkas from the Acarnanian mainland, further to the south peninsulas and small islands on the horizon create borders. One of these islands is *Skórpios*, the private island of the Onassis family. The only noteworthy village on the rest of the coast is the beautiful *Vassilikí* in a wide bay in the south-west.

Towards the Ionian Sea the bay is bordered by the *Lefkáta Peninsula* with a coastline of high white chalk cliffs that drop off into the sea. The coastline is dotted with idyllic sandy coves such as *Pórto*

Interplay of sea and land: from the dunes in the north to the chalk cliffs in the south – a paradise for beach lovers

Katsíki while at other spots there are miles of isolated beaches that difficult to reach. Those seeking peace and quiet on the island (35 km/21 miles long and 15 km/9 miles wide) will find it in the mountain villages high above the west coast and in the interior of the island. Here there are also some lovely hikes. Léfkas does not have a lot to offer those looking for educational trips, little remains of the ancient town founded by Corinth that was founded here in 640 BC and there is also hardly anything from the Venetian era,

due to the 25 earthquakes that have ravaged the island since the 15th century. However, those who are in search of some beautiful beaches will feel right at home on the island.

SIGHTSEEING & PLACES

ÁGIOS NIKÍTAS (124 B2) (*🛱 C4*)

The only seaside resort (pop. 110) right on the west coast by the open sea is nestled in a valley so narrow that there is only enough space for a (pedestrian) street.

The Monastery of Faneroménis offers a shady courtyard to take respite from the heat

The beach in front of the resort is only about 50 m/164 ft long; a longer sandy beach stretches to the north. It is especially popular with tourists with camper vans.

INSIDER TIP **ARCHAEOLOGICAL MUSEUM**
● (124 C1) (*𝄞 D3*)
Modern museum in the cultural centre of Léfkas, where temporary exhibitions are also held. The museum exhibits finds from the archaeological excavations on the island and many of the exhibits are well explained.

The first cabinet, right next to the cashier, showcases ancient music. Four movable terracotta dolls from the graves of 5th century BC children are on show in Hall C. There are also stone urns and tomb monuments and a small part of the ancient cemetery has been reconstructed. Hall D is dedicated to the German archaeologist Wilhelm Dörpfeld and his findings.

Tue–Sun 8am–3pm | admission 2 euros | Lefkáda | Odós Ang. Sikelianoú/Odós N. Svorónou (at the northern end of the coast road)

KALAMÍTSI (124 C3) (*𝄞 C4*)
The small inland village (pop. 200) above the long sandy beach of *Káthisma* lies 380 m/1246 ft above the west coast. On the one hand it is very rural: chickens, goats and donkeys walk freely through the gardens and fields, the whole village seems rustic and messy. On the other hand there are also a number of guesthouses and private rooms, a few tavernas and even a modern café club where, unfortunately, they play music a bit too loudly, even during the day.

KARIÁ (124 B2–3) (*𝄞 D4*)
The largest mountain village (pop. 1000) on the island still has many traditional houses. The village square is shaded by

old plane trees and has a good taverna, and is full of life in late afternoon. At the top end of the village there is also a small, private *ethnological museum (daily 9am–9pm)*, and a private museum mainly exhibiting old record players on the main road *(open when the owner is there)*.

MONASTERY OF FANEROMÉNIS
(124 C1) (*𝄞 D3*)

The only monastery on the island that is still inhabited lies in a small grove above the lagoon and the town. It has recently been extensively restored and now also includes a beautiful garden and a small, but fine monastery museum. The evening services that take place every Wednesday between 8.45pm and 0.45am are particularly atmospheric. *Closed daily 2pm–4pm | 4 km/2.4 miles above Lefkáda on the road to Ágios Nikítas*

LEFKÁDA ★ (124 C1) (*𝄞 D3*)
MAP INSIDE BACK COVER The special charm of the island's capital (pop. 7000) lies in its position – between the lagoon and narrow strait that separates Léfkas from the mainland. The alleys of the town are lined with houses that survived the 1953 earthquake because their upper storeys were built in the Turkish tradition with wood rather than stone. These wooden facades are unfortunately often clad in sheets of metal or synthetic materials giving the island's capital a rather temporary feel.

However, many of its streets and alleys are newly paved and attractive, and many facades are painted in various pastel shades giving it an authentic Mediterranean or even Caribbean look. A few churches from the Venetian era have been preserved although they are marred by some truly ugly bell towers that were replaced after the 1953 quake. The social centre of the town is the *platía* with its kiosks and cafés. Here, to the right of the Ágios Spirídonis church, is the start of *Odós Dimarhou Verrióti* with its authentic handcraft workshops – from coffin makers to icon painters and even dental technicians – and you can watch them at work through the window. The main shopping streets are the largely pedestrian *Odós Derpfeld* and its extension that ends at the street market *Odós Méla*, commonly referred to as *agorá*, market alley. In the summer, the many café bars along the fishing harbour embankment are busy in the evening.

LEFKÁTA PENINSULA
(124 A5–6) (*𝄞 C6–7*)

The white chalk cliffs of the Lefkáta Peninsula offer some of the most beautiful coastal scenery in Greece. The road ends at ★ *Cape Doukáto* where a solitary lighthouse overlooks the ships that constantly pass by on the route between Italy and the Gulf of Pátras. In antiquity this was also the site of a Temple of Apollo. Every year on the Apollo feast day

The waterfall at Nídri only flows from autumn to spring

a condemned man was thrown from the cape strapped with bird wings – those who survived were freed. According to legend, it was here that Sappho, the first female poet in world literature, committed suicide.

Between Athaní and the Cape Doukáto another road branches off to the bay of ★ *Pórto Katsíki,* a pale strip of beach beneath a white chalk cliff. This lovely beach often appears on posters promoting Greek tourism. From Athaní there are roads and tracks leading to several other excellent beaches.

INSIDER TIP ▶ MONÍ ASÓMATON
(124 C3) (*ℳ D5*)

The island's atmospheric ruins of the so-called Monastery of the Archangels (signposted as the "Monastery of the Taxiárches") are situated in a secluded forest setting. Built in the 17th century, the monastery was once home to dozens of monks. The tiny chapel has been preserved but is closed to the public. High walls and archways are what remain of the other buildings with two clearly discernible cisterns. You won't find a nicer picnic spot on the whole of the island. *Signposted on the road from Kariá to Vafkéri in a left-hand bend shortly before reaching Vafkéri | Freely accessible to the public*

NIDRÍ (124 C3) (*ℳ D5*)

The liveliest holiday resort on the island (and also its main ferry terminal) is scenically situated opposite several islets at the entrance to the green fringed Bay of Vlichó. Its bustling centre is the harbour, where car ferries depart for Meganísi, Ithaca and Kefaloniá. This is also where you can find excursion boats to the Onassis island of Skórpios, trips around the island and cruises to other Ionian Islands. There is a modern INSIDER TIP ▶ *monument* to Aristotle Onassis (1906–75) the famous Greek shipping magnate, billionaire and husband of Jacqueline Kennedy.

Take a beautiful hike from Nidrí to the *waterfall* that is situated 3 km/1.8 mile from here in a small, narrow gorge, which only has water until May. There couldn't be a larger choice of daily boat excursions in Greece. The ● "Three beaches" tour is particularly special and takes you to the beautiful Ekrémni beach on the west coast which can only be accessed from the sea since the earthquake in 2014 *(can be booked at Borsalino Travel in Nidrí, see p. 62).*

SANTA MAURA ●
(124 C1) (*D–E3*)
Built in 1684, this fortress is located at the northern canal exit surrounded by shallow wetlands where flocks of flamingos come to graze between September and mid-May.

SIVÓTA
(124 C5) (*D6*)
The former fishing village on a narrow, sheltered bay is especially charming at night, when dozens of yachts anchor here. On the fjord-like bay there are only tiny pebble beaches but there are numerous fish tavernas and bars right on the shore all lying in wait for the wealthy evening public.

INSIDER TIP ▶ VASSILIKÍ
(124 B5) (*C6*)
There are still a few old houses in this village (pop. 370) on the inside of a wide bay that is ideal for windsurfers. The waterfront is lined by countless restaurants shaded by tall eucalyptus trees and a long pebble beach starts right at the edge of the village. The port is under extension and will probably be worth visiting again after 2018. You can now still sail from the quayside to the sandy beaches on the Lefkáta Peninsula.

FOOD & DRINK

FRÍNI STO MÓLO (124 C1) (*D3*)
Fríni, the proprietress, might be the quickest and snappiest restaurant owner of the island. In the kitchen, she displays her creativity, preparing, for example, a lentil salad with *savóro,* a marinated fish served cold. *Lefkáda | Odós Golémos 12 (on the coastal road opposite the pier)* | *Moderate*

LIGHTHOUSE (124 C1) (*D3*)
A small, well-established taverna with a sheltered garden where you can sit quietly and enjoy delicious Greek specialities. Host Sotíris spent some time in Washington D.C. and speaks excellent English.

LOW BUDGET

To see where Onassis and family spent their money, you need not book a boat trip around Skórpios. You can also see the island up close, but without a swim, if you take the Meganísi ferry which passes very close to Skórpios. This way, the return trip will only coast approx. 4.50 euros and you can even visit Meganísi.

The *House of Garden (on the main road | tel. 26 45 03 34 65 | www.houseofgarden.gr)* in the village of *Drépano* is perfect for those who are exploring the island by car or by bike and want to stay near the best of the island's beaches on the Lefkáta Peninsula. A small double room costs 25 euros in May and 40 euros in August. Apartments are available from between 40 and 60 euros.

Reservations are recommended. *Daily from 5pm | Lefkáda | Odós Filarmonikís 14 | tel. 26 45 02 51 17 | Moderate*

LIOTRÍVI (124 C5) (*ⓜ D6*)
Housed in a former olive mill at the southeast end of the promenade at Sivóta, this bar offers the perfect relaxed place in the afternoon to watch the yachtsmen coming into the port who then often come here to celebrate in the evening. *From 8am*

NAUTILOS (124 C1) (*ⓜ D3*)
Here you can sit in the evening surrounded by authentic Greek life with children playing and a hurdy-gurdy player who goes around the tables serenading guests. Pizza, pasta and traditional Greek dishes are served with a twist: *juvétsi* is served in a clay pot pumpkin and *souvláki* on skewers over a wooden board. *Lefkáda | Kentrikí Platía | Budget*

INSIDER TIP OÁSIS ⚘ (124 A5) (*ⓜ C6*)
Forest taverna with tables under the trees. Lamb and goat from their own butchery, homemade cheese. *On the road, 8 km/5 miles from Athaní to Pórto Katsíiki | Moderate*

INSIDER TIP O PLÁTANOS
(124 C3) (*ⓜ D5*)
Garden taverna owned by an Athenian dentist and amateur chef. Lamb and pork chops are sold according to weight, specialities are roast lamb and lamb liver. *Evenings only | Vafkéri | at the church on the main road | Moderate*

PIRÁTES (124 C1) (*ⓜ D3*)
In case the youngsters feel they have to break away from the family holiday for a time: This boat bar, fitted into two decks of a sailing ship replica, s your anchor by day and by night. During the day, távli

and Monopoly are played, in the evenings they play the right music. *Lefkáda*

INSIDER TIP RÁCHI ⚘ ⚘
(124 B2) (*ⓜ C4*)
This venue impresses with its terrace with fantastic views of the sea and the coastal hamlet of Kalamítsi. Wine and oil comes from their own harvest, the many legumes on offer are cultivated in the immediate vicinity. In midsummer you will need to make a reservation. *Exanthia | at the entrance to the village | tel. 26 45 09 94 39 | Budget*

INSIDER TIP SÉSOULAS ⚘
(124 A4) (*ⓜ C5*)
Hostess Georgiá serves her guests vegetables and salads from her own garden, even the chickens are from her coop and the meat is also local. With simple peasant dishes, such as *pastítsio* or stuffed tomatoes and peppers, Sélousas is so authentic that it feels like the Greece of yesteryear. *Drágano | along the main road | Budget*

SHOPPING

DIONÍSIS KONTÓS (124 C1) (*ⓜ D3*)
While men can only worry for their wives' safety, Greek women are literally head over heels in love with this traditional style of shoe. *Lefkáda | Odós Melá 116*

PANAJÓTIS FRANGOÚLIS
(124 C1) (*ⓜ D3*)
The shop is also a distillery and the oúzo, brandy and various liqueurs that you can buy here are also produced on site. *Lefkáda | Odós Mitropóleos 4*

POLYCHRONÓPOULOS
(124 C1) (*ⓜ D3*)
Looking for a local delicacy as a souvenir? Léfkada is famous in Greece for its air-

Kite surfers flying high above Léfkas Beach

dried salami. You can buy it straight from the manufacturer here – for your next picnic or simply to enjoy back home. *Lefkáda | Odós Melá 180*

QUATTRO LINEA
(124 C1) (*ω D3*)

Vivienne Westwood, the mother of punk fashion, surprisingly showcases her collection in Léfkas. *Lefkáda | Odós Melá 114*

STAVRÁKAS
(124 C1) (*ω D3*)

The Stavrákas family has been making Lefkadian sweets for more than 55 years. You absolutely have to try the fig salami made with dried figs, honey, nuts, sesame and spices as well as the sugar-free chocolate with prunes. *Lefkáda | Odós Derpfeld 22 | www.stavrakas-shop.com*

SPORTS & BEACHES

Léfkas is a Mecca for wind and kite surfers, especially at Lefkáda and Vassilikí (see p. 103). The best address for parasailing, aterski and wakeboarding ist *Dennis Watersports Centre (mobile tel. 69 32 15 46 25)* at the northern end of Nidrí.

The most beautiful beaches are situated on the spit of Lefkáda north of the lagoon, on the Bay of Vassilikí and below Athaní on the Lefkáta Peninsula (Pórto Katsíki, Gialós and Egrémni Beach). Very popular beaches include Ágios Nikítas and Káthisma and the beach 5 km/3 miles below the village of Póros on the south coast. Less frequented is the pebble beach of Mílos which one can reach on foot from Ágios Nikítas (25 minutes).

ENTERTAINMENT

Dance club lovers will be disappointed on Léfkas as the club selection is very limited. The liveliest (also during the day) is the outdoor disco café, the *Sail-Inn (Nidrí | on the beach towards Lefkáda)* and in the music bar *Roadhouse (Nidrí |*

Mojito instead of ouzo –
celebrating, Lefkáda style

at the southern end of the main thoroughfare). In the island's capital the youth meet up in *Kárma (Lefkáda | Odós Derpfeld 1)* and *Club Pure (Odós Ang. Sikelianoú 4)* on the promenade. In the summer, Greek live music is often played at the *Capital Club* on the shore north of the Archaeological Museum.

Perhaps inspired by the town's slightly Caribbean feeling, a kind of Caribbean club culture has established itself in Lefkáda. A salsa party is held every evening in summer at the *Cubana Salsa Bar (Odós Verióti 6/Pinélopis 4)* which has twelve types of mojitos on its cocktail menu as well as different rums and a wide selection of cigars. Refreshing mojito twists are also served in the *Octopus' Garden* wine bar *(Odós Mitrolpóleos 19)*, including one mixed with ouzo and another with the Greek liquor mastícha.

WHERE TO STAY

CASA CAMPOS (124 C1) (*D3*)
Three double-storey studios for 2–4 persons in each of the four houses painted in colourful Ionian colours. The maisonettes are set in over an acre garden with old olive trees and a large swimming pool. Modern, 10–15 minutes to the town centre and to the beaches, open all year round. *Lefkáda | south-west of the town | mobile tel. 69 83 76 46 05 | www. casacampos.gr | Moderate–Expensive*

EVA BEACH (124 C3) (*D5*)
Owned and run by the family of the village baker, this beachside hotel is situated to the north of the port; the bar on its shady overgrown terrace is a popular meeting spot for the many regular guests. *30 rooms, 14 apartments. | Nidrí | tel. 26 45 09 25 45 | www.evabeach.gr | Moderate*

FANTÁSTICO ⚘ (124 B3) (*C4*)
Studios and apartments for 2–5 persons on a fantastic hillside location with sea views. *8 apartments | Kalamítsi | on the town outskirts | tel. 26 45 09 93 90 | www. fantastico.gr | Budget*

LÉFKAS ⚘ (124 C1) (*D3*)
Largest hotel in the island's capital, at the start of the causeway to the mainland. Three-storey, modern finishes, most of the rooms have sea views. *93 rooms | Lefkáda | Odós Panagoú 2 | tel. 26 45 02 39 16 | www.hotel-lefkas.gr | Moderate*

ODÉON ⚘
(124 B5) (*C6*)
Modern studios and apartments with balconies and beautiful views, in a house with a swimming pool, right on the beach and 800 m/875 yd from the town

centre. *17 apartments | Vassilikí | off the road towards Komílio | tel. 26 45 03 19 18 | www.vassiliki.com | Budget–Moderate*

INSIDER TIP **PIROFÁNI**
(124 C1) (*Ø D3*)

Modern guesthouse, centrally located, good value for money, friendly host family. All rooms with balconies, air conditioning and fridges. *18 rooms | Lefkáda | Odós Derpfeld 36 | tel. 26 45 02 58 44 | www.pirofanilefkada.gr | Budget*

PORTO KATSIKI STUDIOS ☆
(124 A4) (*Ø C5*)

The complex lies in a beautiful, scenic location and offers rooms and studios for up to four persons, good parking options and a small garden. Excellent value for money! *8 rooms | Athaní | at the lower end of town | tel. 26 45 03 31 36 | www.portokatsikistudios.com | Budget*

INSIDER TIP **ROUDA BAY**
(124 C5) (*Ø D6*)

The complex features buildings with natural stone, tiled roofs and many also with typical Lefkadian wooden facades. It is set in a truly paradisiacal garden, each suite different, and all are furnished to a high standard. The maisonettes offer accommodation for up to 6 persons. *28 rooms | Póros | on the coast road | tel. 26 45 09 56 34 | www.roudabay.gr | Moderate*

SOFIAS STUDIOS ☆
(124 C5) (*Ø D6*)

The six simply decorated studios, owned by the friendly and helpful hostess Sofía, lie right above a small beach, almost all have sea views. *Sivóta | on the small road above the bay | tel. 26 45 02 53 53 | www.sofia-studios.com| Budget*

FOR BOOKWORMS AND FILM BUFFS

The Odyssey – The more than 2700 year old Homeric epic is available in several English editions, in both verse and prose form. It is also available in a series of audio CDs. "The Odyssey" has also been made into a film many times, such as by Mario Camerini with Kirk Douglas and Silvana Mangano (1954, 2 DVDs) and as a TV series with Armand Assante and Greta Scacchi (1997, DVD)

Odysseus and Penelope: An Ordinary Marriage – An entertaining novel by the classicist Inge Merkel (translated by Renate Latimer) that retells the myth from an unusual perspective

Captain Corelli's Mandolin – The best selling novel by Louis de Bernières was also made into a film by John Madden (2001) starring Nicolas Cage and Penelope Cruz. The novel is set in Kefaloniá during the Second World War

My Map of You – This novel (2016) by Isabelle Broom is set on Zákynthos and makes for a great summer read: Holly, the heroine, has to discover a family secret on the island, but must also think about her own life. Of course, romance and the beautiful scenery play their parts in this, too...

Available from the private travel agencies in Lefkáda, Nidrí and Vassilikí. For information about ferries, the best is *Borsalino Travel (Nidrí | between the thoroughfare and the harbour | tel. 26 45 09 25 28 | www.borsalinotravel.gr)*.

The official island website is *www.lefkada.gr*

WHERE TO GO

KÁLAMOS (125 E–F 4–6) (*ØII F–G6*)

The small island (only 9 square miles but up to 785 m/2575 ft high in parts) has a population of 250 and is almost car-free. There are three tavernas in the main harbour village of *Kálamos* and some small pebble beaches in the hamlet of *Episkopí*. Regular connections to Mítikas (mainland) and in the summer some trips are organised to Kálamos from Lefkáda. You can overnight in a few private rooms.

KASTÓS (125 E–F 5–6) (*ØII F6–7*)

This tiny island (just 3 square miles with a population of 40) is entirely car-free. There are two tavernas and very basic accommodation in the community hall in the island's only village. Several small sandy beaches are accessible on foot. Regular ferry connections are available between the island and Mítikas (mainland). In the summer there are sometimes excursion boats from Lefkáda.

MEGANÍSI ★ (125 D4–5) (*ØII E5–6*)

Meganísi (pop. 500) is the largest of the islets between Léfkas and the mainland. The billionaire Lord Jacob Rothschild has bought 500 hectares in the island's south where he hopes to entice other billionaires to build unique, exclusive villas there too. However, for now, the island

is open to everyone. Most ferries stop at *Pórto Spília* harbour. A 10 minute walk leads to the pretty inland village of *Spartochóri*, a further 60 minutes to the second village, *Katoméri*. The most comfortable accommodation so far is the *Esperídes Resort (50 rooms | tel. 26 45 05 17 61 | www.esperides-resort.gr | Expensive)* between Pórto Spiliá and Spartochóri, there is also the family friendly hotel *Meganísi (35 rooms | tel. 26 45 05 12 40 | www.ionianislandholidays.com | Moderate)* in Katoméri.

NIKÓPOLIS ★ (0) (*ØII D–E1*)

Impressive remains from antiquity are just 9 km/5.5 miles from Préveza on the mainland. The site is easily reached by bus from Léfkas. The trip is worthwhile even for those who are not particularly interested in archaeology.

Nikópolis was founded in 30 BC by Octavian, the future Roman Emperor Augustus, to commemorate his naval victory over Anthony and Cleopatra and it was settled until the 13th century. The city enjoyed its heyday during the early Byzantine period in the years between AD 500 and 600. Some of the foundation walls, stone carvings and mosaic floors of the basilicas dating to that era have been preserved. The most impressive of the remains are, however, the Byzantine city walls with its well preserved gates and towers. Even the amphitheatre is testimony to the size of the city, despite its destroyed terraces *(most of the excavations of the Byzantine city are open to the public, excavations of the ancientc city daily 8am–3pm | admission 2 euros)*.

In the small *excavation museum (Tue–Fri 8.30am–3pm, Sat/Sun 8am–3pm | admission 3 euros)* at the edge of the Doumetios Basilica there are Roman sculptures, glasses and coins. *Museum and excavations are on the main Préveza–Arta road | buses from Préveza*

to Préveza (21 km/13 miles away) run several times daily

PRÉVEZA (0) *(🗺 E2)*

Préveza (pop. 15,000) is a small town surrounded by the sea on three sides, with a hint of the Orient. It is located at

SKÓRPIOS (124–125 C–D4) *(🗺 E5)*

The former private island of the Onassis family, now owned by Ekaterina Rybelovleva, the daughter of a Russian

Visit Meganísi sooner rather than later, before you have to pay an entrance fee

the mouth of the Ambracian Gulf, which stretches from here over 35 km/22 miles inland. An undersea tunnel was built under the mouth of the gulf connecting the town to the mainland.

On the other side of the gulf mouth a small fort marks the site of ancient *Actium*, which gave the sea battle its name. This decisive battle with Anthony and Cleopatra on the one hand and Octavian on the other hand, occurred in 31 BC, far out at sea.

A stroll through the main shopping street and the small market hall is worthwhile. Many of the houses date back to the 19th century; in the *Ágios Athanássios* church there are some murals. *Buses from Lefkáda*

magnate, is not open to the public. But you can view the island's private beaches and the rooftops of the houses by boat. On a trip around the island you imagine the lifestyle of the shipping magnate who lived here, first with the opera diva Maria Callas and then with Jackie Onassis. Excursion boats are even permitted to dock at one of the island's beaches.

VÓNITSA (0) *(🗺 F2)*

A well preserved Venetian Turkish *castle* towers over the small town (pop. 3800) on the southern side of the Ambracian Gulf. *Castle open to the public | buses from Lefkáda to Vónitsa (22 km/14 miles away) several times daily*

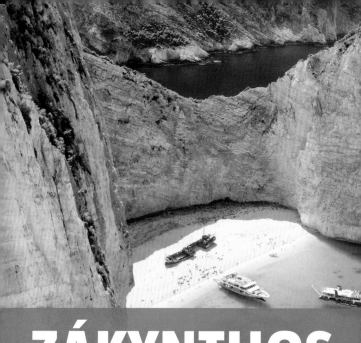

ZÁKYNTHOS

The Venetians called their southernmost property in the Ionian Sea *Fior di Levante*, "the flower of the Levant". The 157 square mile island was noted by the Italians for its fertility, its good wines, the lovely landscape and the aristocratic beauty of the island capital. Its beaches held little attraction to them.

However, today's visitors to the island come especially for the good sandy beaches. The most beautiful, those on the Bay of Laganás, have been sought out since time immemorial by sea turtles who visit to lay their eggs. During the 1980s tourism took root and a conflict of interest resulted in a bitter struggle between hotel developers and nature conservation. On the one side there were those wanting more hotels, apartments, tavernas and shops along the beaches while the other side wanted the whole bay to be declared a national park and called for a tourism boycott of the island. Finally a compromise was reached.

The *Bay of Laganás* was declared a marine national park 20 years ago. The beach of Sekaniá on the western side of the *Skopós Peninsula* is entirely off limits to the public. No boats may sail on the other beaches on the western side. In the remaining Bay of Laganás, the speed for motor boats is limited to six to eight knots; in the triangle between Laganás, Límni Kerioú and the small islet of Marathonísi boats may not anchor or berth. Bathing is still permitted on the tourist beaches. The national park administration also have information

The flower of the Levant: a fertile island caught between nature conservation and tourism development

stands where people can educate themselves about the correct behaviour for welfare of the sea turtles.

Zákynthos is just as attractive for holiday-makers as it is for sea turtles. The centre of the island's capital is charming with large and small squares and its elongated position, between the sea and a low range of the Bocháli hills ensures that the area stays contained. The bizarre rocks of the 492 m/1614 ft high summit of Mount Skopós create a prominent fixture on the horizon.

The island is clearly delineated, with a range of hills along the west and east coast. In the east the hills are green and low, in the west they rise up to a height of 756 m/2480 ft. The wide plain between them is intensively farmed and it is where the majority of island villages are located. In between the villages are country estates which are reminiscent of Tuscany with their beautiful gates and long driveways. In contrast to this lush fertility, large sections of the mountain area in the west only have woods or fields

How many bridges like the one in Argássi do we have to cross to get ahead?

here and there. While the east coast is largely fringed by a narrow strip of sandy beach, in the west the coast drops sharply into the sea almost on its entire length. In some places there are still pristine sandy beaches such as *Shipwreck Beach,* which can only be reached by boat.

The approx. 39,000 Zákynthos locals are viewed as cheerful people. They celebrate carnival more intensively than any of other Ionian islanders – and they sing more often. Their typical songs are the more Italianate *kantádes* that have nothing in common with the folk music on the Aegean Islands and the mainland of Greece that are strongly influenced by the Orient. Even as a tourist you can learn *kantádes*: they are sung in many tavernas on the summer evenings.

SIGHTSEEING & PLACES

INSIDER TIP **AGALÁS** (130 C5) (*Ø E18*)

In the centre of the remote village a sign-post indicates the mile long way to the Venetian Wells (or *Andrónios Wells*); eleven well preserved cisterns from the Venetian era. They are ideally situated within a valley lined with vineyards *(open to the public; follow the signs from the village and at the junction continue straight ahead until the asphalt ends).*

On the way to the cisterns, on the opposite side of the valley, you will see a cave opening in the rock; you can visit the cave on the way back. The double storey cave called *Spíleo tou Damianoú* is 200 m/218 yds from the car park, the beautiful route there is part of the attraction. In the village centre it is worth stopping off at the *Art Gallery (only open sporadically)* which is on the main road towards Kilioméno.

ÁGIOS NIKÓLAOS/SKINÁRI
(130 B2) *(ࣿ D15)*

The little village on the Bay of Skinári only has 30 permanent residents, but is the second most important harbour on the island. This is where the excursion boats leave for the Blue Caves and Shipwreck Beach, and also where car ferries depart twice daily for Pessáda on Kefaloniá. The village sand and pebble beach is only a few hundred feet long.

ALIKÉS *(130 C3) (ࣿ E16)*

This coastal village is particularly popular with British holidaymakers. It is only sparsely developed and lies in on the edge of a disused salt flat right on a miles long, narrow sandy beach. In the evening there are almost more horse-drawn carriages than cars on the road and the prices here are remarkably low. The small fishing port at the mouth of the river is especially charming. Approximately 150 m/492 ft upstream a six-arched Venetian era bridge spans the river.

INSIDER TIP ÁNO GERAKÁRI
(131 D3) *(ࣿ E16)*

The ☀ courtyard of the *Ágios Nikólaos* church is the highest point of this inland village and it offers a good view over the island. It is best to leave your car at the village entrance as there is hardly any parking space in the village and at the top at the church.

ARGÁSSI (131 E4) *(ࣿ F17)*

Another holiday resort that is popular among British tourists, it stretches along a narrow, sandy beach and the main road on the Skopós Peninsula and also sprawls even further inland. From here the view of Zákynthos Town is lovely. A INSIDER TIP *three arched bridge* from 1803, when the island was under British administration, confirms that Argássi was established well before the days of mass tourism. The ruined bridge is on the beach in front of the Xénos Kamára Beach Hotel (from the centre 30 m behind the petrol station).

⭐ **Blue Caves (Galázia Spílea)**
A magical swim in a beautiful cave
→ p. 68

⭐ **Bocháli**
Pine trees within ruined medieval walls and fantastic views from the cliff → p. 68

⭐ **Loúcha**
Ancient village far from the beaten tourist track → p. 71

⭐ **Shipwreck Beach (Navagíou)**
A beautiful and isolated cove, with a shipwreck on the beach, which can only be reached by boat
→ p. 73

⭐ **Zákynthos Museum**
The Ionian Islands style of painting
→ p. 74

⭐ **Varkaróla**
Genuine Zakynthian *kantádes* sung every evening → p. 79

⭐ **Apeláti**
Modern guesthouse and taverna in the middle of olive trees and vineyards → p. 80

⭐ **Olympia**
Ancient sanctuary and sport complex – the place where the Olympic Games originated
→ p. 81

MARCO POLO HIGHLIGHTS

BLUE GROTTOS (GALÁZIA SPÍLEA) ★
(130 B1) (*∅ D15*)

The Blue Grottos of Zákynthos are every bit as beautiful as their namesakes in Capri. You enter by boat, gliding through natural rock portals and bizarre formations into the crystal clear, blue and turquoise shimmering water of the grottos where you can take a swim. Excursion boats to the caves depart regularly from

(May–Oct daily 8am–2.30pm | admission 3 euros), which is almost completely overgrown with pine trees, forming a real forest. The outer walls and the gates are well preserved, but little remains of the other buildings such as the storerooms, churches and barracks.

After visiting the fortress you can take a stroll (400 m/437 yd) to the village main square, which is above the steep

Bocháli: panoramic dining with ultimate views of the port below

Ágios Nikólaos/Skinári and from the pier below the lighthouse at Cape Skinári. There are also boat trips from Zákynthos Town and from Makrís Gialós.

BOCHÁLI ★ ☼
(131 D–E4) (*∅ F16*)

The village on the elongated range of hills above the island capital is the ideal destination during the late afternoon and early evening. First you can visit the sprawling Venetian *fortress Bocháli*

slope of the hill range. The view over the town, the harbour and the Peloponnese is terrific. *Paid parking on the village street*

ÉXO CHÓRIA
(130 B3) (*∅ D16*)

The village *platía*, with its massive ancient plane tree, lies on the island's circular road. From here you can also reach over two dozen Venetian cisterns (just over a hundred feet away), which are in a field beside the main road towards Volimés. However, they are not as well preserved as those in Agalás.

KALAMÁKI
(131 E4) (*m̄ F17*)

Kalamáki has a sandy beach just as beautiful as that of the neighbouring Laganás, but it is far quieter. Hotels and guesthouses line the 200 m/656 ft village street and are also scattered in the fields surrounding Kalamáki.

KALIPÁDO
(131 D3) (*m̄ E16*)

The village is home to the island's largest private wine cellar: *Callínico (Mon–Sat 9am–8pm | signposted entrance on the main road from Zákynthos Town)*. Here you can not only enjoy a free wine tasting and buy wine, but you can also see a small exhibition that includes historic machinery, oak barrels, a wine press and the baskets in which the grapes used to be carried.

KAMBÍ ⚜
(130 B4) (*m̄ D17*)

Kambí is a village that is popular with tourists who come to enjoy the sunset and see the steep cliff. A large cross at this cliff commemorates the unknown number of left wing partisans who were thrown into the sea by their right wing opponents during the Greek Civil War in 1944. On the left hand side of the road that leads from the village up to the cross, are some shaft tombs from the Mycenaean period.

KERÍ/LÍMNI KERIOÚ

Kerí (131 D6) (*m̄ E18*) is a picturesque mountain village (pop. 550) that is untouched by tourism, with quaint *kafenía*, that also double as grocery stores. The *Panagía tis Keriótissas* church has an impressive bell tower and a wooden carved iconostasis dating to 1745.

From the village centre a road leads 2 km/1.2 mile to the lighthouse at ⚜ *Cape Kerí*. The view from here over the 100 m/328 ft high cliff is magnificent. In the harbour village *Límni Kerioú* (131 D5) (*m̄ E–F18*), the diving centre of the island, is worth seeing for the ● *Herodotus Spring*, a source of both water and pitch. You can collect some yourself with the sticks provided. The short pebble beach of Límni Kerioú is ideal for a swim and every hour boat trips depart from the harbour to the cliffs and sea caves of Kerí. Another option to explore the steep coastline is to take out one of the more than 100 motor boats lined up here in summer. You don't even need a boat licence to sail one.

LOW BUDGET

In Zákynthos Town the best place for an inexpensive and delicious meal is the taverna *O Koúzis*, founded in 1890. There is no menu and no outdoor seating, however they have a handful of fresh dishes daily from 5 to 6 euros, such as spaghetti with meat sauce or bean stew. And a litre of wine only costs 5 euros. *Mon–Fri noon–4pm | Odós Tertséti 54*

The cheapest boat trips to the Blue Grottos and Shipwreck Beach depart from the lighthouse at the most north-eastern tip. The boats leave for the caves every 10–15 minutes and to Shipwreck Beach several times a day (tour to the Blue Grotto 7.50 euros, to both the grotto and Shipwreck Beach 15 euros).

MONASTERY OF ÁGIOS GEORGÍOU KREMNÓN (130 A2) (*D15–16*)

Secluded monastery in a forest near to the cliff coast that looks just like a fortress. Until recently, only a lone monk still lived here, now the monastery is completely deserted. Its high walls hide a fortified tower with several 16th century pitch chutes and a beautiful monastery church with an 18th century baroque interior. Opposite the entrance to the monastery are four new bells in an olive tree, each labelled with the names of their donors.

MONASTERY OF ANAFONITRÍA (130 A3) (*D16*)

Uninhabited monastery on the outskirts of Anafonitría village has its entrance through a massive 15th century tower gate that is overgrown with caper shrubs. The yellow Byzantine flag with the black double-headed eagle flies from the tower. The monastery church with frescoes from the 17th century is well preserved, and you can see the old oven and olive press used by the monks. The monastery was home to the island saint Dioissios in his last years as abbot. During this time he proved true Christian brotherly love: he offered his brother's murderer asylum in the monastery. *Cloisters open to the public, church May–Sept daily 9am–1pm | free admission*

KORÍTHI (130 B1) (*D15*)

From the northernmost village of the island, a narrow asphalt road leads to *Cape Skinári* in the extreme north of the island. From the short quay below the lighthouse there are boat trips offered to the Blue Caves and Shipwreck Beach, where no big tour groups will be onn board.

LAGANÁS (131 D5) (*F17*)

The main holiday resort destination of the island (along with neighbouring Kalamáki with which it is growing together) is near to the airport flight path. Tourists using the beautiful sandy beach without paying attention to the strict requirements of the conservationists are a threat to the existence of the loggerhead sea turtle and as a result some of

MORE THAN 1000 NESTS

Loggerhead turtles *(Caretta caretta)* have been digging their nests on the sandy beaches of the Bay of Laganás since time immemorial. From June to August they come ashore in the evening to lay up to 120 ping pong ball size eggs before covering them with sand and heading back to the sea. A turtle can lay eggs up to three times during this time. After about 60 days the offspring hatch – again at night – and then immediately make their way to the sea. They orientate themselves by the starlight that is reflected on the water. Tourism however, threatens the turtles in various ways. Umbrellas stuck into the sand can destroy the eggs; nocturnal activities on the beach can prevent the mothers from laying their eggs. The newly hatched offspring may be guided in the wrong direction by lights close to the beach. They are then spotted by predators and snatched up or they dry out in the sun during the day.

the large tour operators no longer offer Laganás as a destination. Nevertheless, the settlements keep spreading along the beach and deeper into the hinterland. The long main street that leads from the beach into the town is packed with bars and music clubs and even has the island's first McDonald's. There is a strong British presence, on Sundays restaurants offer Sunday roasts with Yorkshire pudding, in the bars guests are entertained with quiz sessions, karaoke and sport on big screens.

LITHÁKIA
(131 D5) (*M E–F17*)

The hamlet in the south of the island is worth a short stop to visit the ● *Aristeon Olive Press.* A family member is on hand to explain the long history of the company and the manufacturing process, and you can also do a tasting and purchase some of their organic oil. *Daily 9am–5pm*

LOÚCHA ★
(130 C4) (*M E17*)

This village, on the edge of a mountain valley, is only inhabited by a few elderly residents. It escaped damage in the 1953 earthquake and even its newer buildings have done little to change its authentic feel. It remains a good example of what Zakynthian villages looked like more than 50 years ago.

MACHERÁDO
(130–131 C–D4) (*M E17*)

The church of *Agía Mávra (daily from sunrise to sunset / free admission)* in the large inland village of Macherádo (pop. 900) is the most important pilgrimage destination on the island. The church was destroyed by fire more than ten years ago, but is now – depending on donations – undergoing renovations. The 16th century icon of St Mávra which was covered

Olives growing under the Greek sun. They are ripe when black

in a sheath of embossed silver in the 19th century survived intact and now miraculous powers are attributed to her. That is why she has numerous votive plaques around her, each one depicts what the faithful have prayed to her for assistance: a child, a house, healthy eyes or limbs, a healthy heart and more.

Above the village, to the left of the road to Kiloméno, is the INSIDER TIP *Panagía i Eleftherótria nunnry (daily 8.30am–noon and 4pm–7pm, when closed ring*

A collector's dream come true: Pigadákia Museum

the bell). It was founded in 1961 and the abbey church has beautiful frescoes painted in the Byzantine style. In an adjoining room a nun shows stones from many biblical locations, such as the Sea of Galilee and the house of Mary in Nazareth. The first abbess of the convent gathered them herself on her travels.

PÁRKO ELIÉS ●
(130 B2) (*ω D15*)

Many Greeks dream of owning their own museum. The farmer and construction site worker Jánnis Gidítsis is one man who has made this dream come true. This passionate collector of rocks, bizarre roots and rusty cars has created a strange paradise for you to visit in a former quarry; in the taverna next door, his wife cooks recipes passed on to her by her grandmother. Daily *9am–7pm | free admission | on the road from Vólimes to Cape Skinári*

PIGADÁKIA
(130 C3) (*ω E16*)

Spíros Vertzágio has been collecting antiquities on the island for 20 years, from household goods to agricultural equipment, and displays everything in his *Folk Museum (daily 9am–9pm | admission 3 euros | on the road to Alikés)*. He also built a traditional treehouse, in the past these served as a resting place for the farmers during the harvest time and even as a place to stay overnight. Spíros also runs a traditional *taverna (Budget)* in the village centre, where he sells local produce such as currants, olive oil and wine.

The sound of splashing water is everywhere in the village as it has numerous springs, including a sulphurous spring under the altar of the small *chapel* opposite the taverna. Believers and the ill draw from the spring. You can get to Pigadákia from Alikés either by horse and carriage or by miniature train (that runs on rubber wheels) that is also owned by Spíros *(the tour takes approx. 2 hours | fare 12 euros)*.

PÓRTO LIMNIÓNA
(130 B4) *(𝄞 D17)*

Getting into the water of the long, narrow fjord-like bay on the west coast is not very easy so after you have had your swim you can regain your strength at the *Pórto Limnióna Taverna (Moderate)* with lovely views out to sea.

PÓRTO RÓCHA
(130 B5) *(𝄞 D17)*

You can reach the Bay of Pórto Rócha either from Pórto Limniónas or from the mountain village of Ágios León. For those brave enough, there is diving board about 5 m/16 ft above the water.

PÓRTO VRÓMI
(130 A3) *(𝄞 C–D16)*

It is believed that Mary Magdalene – according to the Gospel, she was the first to find that Jesus' grave was empty – came to the shore here on her way to Rome. Today the 10 m/30 ft long pebble beach has just a simple beach bar. The surrounding pines almost reach the water's edge. There are several excursion boats in the quay that do trips out to Shipwreck Beach *(incl. 1 hour swimming break | 15 euros/person)*. Pedal boats are also rented out for rides on the fjord *(10 euros/hour)*.

SHIPWRECK BEACH (NAVAGÍOU) ★
(130 A2) *(𝄞 C15–16)*

Images of this beautiful beach are often used to promote Greece all over the world. The remote cove's white, sandy beach is only accessible by boat and lies at the foot of a steep cliff – and in the middle of the beach is the wreck of the freighter that ran aground in the 1970s.

The shimmering water is a deep turquoise, on some days with swirls of white.

You can get to Shipwreck Beach by boat from Pórto Vromí; however your dream photo can only be taken from the edge of the cliff. To get there you have to drive from the Monastery of Ágios Georgíou Kremnón northwards on the asphalt road, turn left after 200 m/218 yd and reach the end of the road after a further 1200 m/3937 ft. There is a small ☂ viewing platform that juts out over the abyss. You can see *Shipwreck Beach* even better from the path that runs to the right of the platform, but this requires you to be brave and have a head for heights.

SKOPÓS PENINSULA
(131 E–F 4–5) *(𝄞 G17)*

The peninsula in the south-east of the island capital has been named after Mount Skopós (492 m/1614 ft) which towers above it. The north of the peninsula is lined with many small bays with sand and pebble beaches and only very few hotels and apartment blocks so far. In the south of the peninsula is the Bay of Laganás with miles of sandy beaches. However, the beaches form part of the nesting area for the loggerhead turtles. Visitors should therefore follow the nature conservationist rules which are written on signs at the beach entrances. A free exhibition centre opposite the car park also provides information about the nature in the national park which you can explore by taking a long walk along the beach at Gerákas.

VÓLIMES
(130 B2) *(𝄞 D15)*

The rambling mountain village in the north of the island looks like a large market during the summer. Everywhere along the roadside there are sellers with "genuinely handmade" embroidered cloths and decorated covers. A few of them actually are the handiwork of Zakynthian women – but the majority of the wares come from workshops on the mainland and are not handmade at all.

ZÁKYNTHOS MUSEUM ★ ●
(130 E4) (*∅ F16–17*)

The museum provides a detailed overview of the history of painting on the Ionian Islands and especially of the works of the so-called Ionian School of the 17–19th century, which was strongly influenced by Italian painting. A relief model and historical photos show what the town looked like before the earthquake in 1953. *Tue–Sun 8am–3pm | admission 4 euros | Zákynthos Town | Platía Solomoú*

ZÁKYNTHOS TOWN
(131 E4) (*∅ F16–17*)
MAP INSIDE BACK COVER

After the earthquake of 1953, Zákynthos Town (pop. 11,000) had to be completely rebuilt. Fortunately the result is not an ugly town in the style of the 1950s, but a good mix of historical reconstruction and appealing new buildings. The only sightseeing options though are the museums, but there are a few interesting churches.

Right on the coast is the large Platía Solomoú and the church of the patron saint of seafarers, the *Ágios Nikólaos*. It was built in 1560 with funding by the local fishermen's guild. On the Platía Agíou Márkou with its many cafés, is the small *San Marcus* church where a Roman Catholic mass takes place every Sunday at 7pm in the summer. The painting above the altar is said to be by Titian or one of his students.

If you walk a few steps east from the Platía Agíou Márkou, you will come across the *Mitrópolis,* the town's cathedral. It is decorated with magnificent frescoes in the traditional Byzantine style. Continue from the Mitrópolis towards the sea, turn left at the first intersection and you will see the very beautiful INSIDER TIP portal of the *Kiría ton Ángelon* church *dating back to* 1687.

At the western end of the coastal road is the largest and most important ● church in town, dedicated to the island saint *Dioníssios*. This church was also repainted in the traditional Byzantine style in the 1980s. Parts of the frescoes depict scenes from the life and work of the saint, who was born on Zákynthos in 1547 and died here in 1622. Especially beautiful are the frescoes on the western wall that represent the history of creation; they were done in 1990 and have a naïve style similar to works by the French painter Henri Rousseau (1844–1910). The western facade is adorned with modern mosaics depicting the patron saints of three Ionian Islands: Saint Spyridon of Corfu, Saint Gerássimos of Kefaloniá and Saint Dioníssios of Zákynthos. The remains of the island's saint are particularly revered and lie in a silver sarcophagus. The magnificent sarcophagus stands in a side chapel to the right of the chancel *(daily 7.30am–1pm and 5pm–7.30pm)*. In the adjoining building is the island's *Bishop's Palace*.

When you return to the town centre, take Odós Tertséti street and on your left hand side you will find a small piece of land where the island's synagogue once stood. It was founded in 1489 by the Jewish community but was destroyed in 1953 by the earthquake. Two *memorials (Odós Tertséti 44)* commemorate the island's Orthodox bishop and the mayor of Zákynthos at time of the German occupation during the Second World War. They bravely resisted the Nazi order to supply a list of their Jewish fellow citizens, and in so doing saved them from evacuation to the German extermination camps.

own vineyard. Occasionally *kantádes* are played in the evening. *June–Sept daily from 7pm, otherwise only Fri–Sun from 7pm | Kilioméno | on the road starting between campanile and church | Expensive*

Not only fishermen cast anchor in front of Zákynthos Town

FOOD & DRINK

ALESTA
(131 E4) (*ØJ F17*)

The wafer-thin pizza crusts at the Alesta restaurant are delicious; their salads are fantastic and the service lives up to the same excellent standards. *Zákynthos Town | Platía Ag. Márkou | Expensive*

INSIDER TIP ALITZERÍNI
(130 C4) (*ØJ E17*)

The taverna, in a traditional two-storey Zakynthian farmhouse, is well known by all the island locals. From the terraces you overlook the hills of the island. The ingredients change daily so there is no menu. The house wine comes from the

FIORO TOU LEVANTE ● 🌿
(130 C3) (*ØJ E16*)

The restaurant is worth visiting for its panoramic view as well as the splendid handicraft work made by the proprietor Mártha for the restaurant's interior. Order a large pizza for two and a salad followed by the Fioro tou Levante cocktail, concocted by owner Gerássimos. *Áno Gerakári | by the church on the summit | Budget*

KÓMIS 🌐 (131 E4) (*ØJ F16–17*)

Probably the island's prettiest fish taverna is situated at the entrance to the ferry pier and is an advocate of the slow food movement. Other than fillet steak, fish dominates the menu with freshly caught fish, sea urchins, smoked eel and stuffed sardines. Starters include the traditional broad-bean dip *fáva* and Zakynthian olives. *Zákynthos Town | by the ferry pier | www.komis-tavern.gr | Expensive*

O KÓKKINOS VRÁCHOS
(131 E4) *(∅ F16–17)*

The town's most elegant coffee shop serves the best coffee and other refresh-

ocean; the small pebble beach in fro of the taverna is also good for swimmir You will be served fish caught that ve morning by Joánna herself, as well meat from the island. During the hi season one or two baked or cooke dishes are also available. *Drossía | 3(m/328 yd north of Hotel Tsámis Moderate*

Take a seat at the Platía Solomoú and soak in the laid-back atmosphere

ing drinks. Even if you choose to sit outside or under the arcades, make sure to catch a glimpse of its stylish interior. *Zákynthos Town | Platía Solomoú (inside the library building) | Moderate*

INSIDER TIP **PÓRTO ROÚLIS**
(131 D3) *(∅ E–F16)*

Host Dioníssos and his wife Katína run one of the most authentic tavernas on the island together with their three daughters Dímitra, Yióta and Joánna. The glassed-in terrace is right next to the

INSIDER TIP **PORTOKÁLI**
(131 E4) *(∅ F17)*

The most unusual restaurant of the islar invites you to drinks as well as extensi meals under the motto *polichóros géfs* ("manifold taste experiences"). The c ourful decor is as unusual as the mer The walls are often decorated with cc temporary art and there are occasic ally live concerts and guest appearanc by British DJs. *Argássi | at the northe town entrance | www.portokalion.gr Moderate*

TO FANÁRI TU KERIOÚ ☘
(130 C6) (𝄞 E18)

Well maintained taverna high above the cliff with dazzling views. Host Stamátis Livéris is actually a construction engineer, but likes to indulge his love of the culinary arts. Some of his specialities include rabbit and chicken stuffed with liver, rice, cheese and vegetables as well as pork belly stuffed with vegetables. *Kerí | 1.5 km/1 mile outside the town, some 150 m from the lighthouse* | Moderate

ZÉPOS
(131 E4) (𝄞 F17)

This taverna with outdoor non-smoking area is run by a young Canadian-born Greek with his feisty wife from London. Its international flair is evident in its excellent service and exceptional cuisine. Recommended is the excellent tomato soup followed by lamb kléftiko and for dessert strawberry cheesecake. A INSIDER TIP rare type of grappa-like Zakynthian alcohol *(tsípouro),* which the owner's father officially makes himself, is also served. *Kalamáki Beach |* Moderate

SHOPPING

ÉLLINON GÉFSIS ☯
(131 E4) (𝄞 F16–17)

The attractively decorated "Greek taste" shop offers culinary delights and cosmetics from all over Greece, including numerous organically grown products. *Zákynthos Town | Odós Alex. Roma 13*

INSIDER TIP HANNE MI'S CERAMIC ART STUDIO ● (131 F5) (𝄞 G17)

The Norwegian artist Hanne Mi, who also worked for the National Park centre, produces ceramic and earthenware of high quality: tiles and fountains, bowls and vases, cups, plates, egg cups, frames –

and of course decorative turtles. She also offers two-hour *pottery classes (Tue and Fri 10am–noon | 20 euros)* as well as private lessons. *Vassilikós | on the main road before the turn-off to Porto Roma Beach | www.ceramichannemi.com*

HELMI & CO (131 E4) (𝄞 F16–17)
Are you interested in finding out what Greek women like to wear? This boutique sells the latest fashions as well as shoes and accessories all made in Greece *(Odós Alex. Róma 99)*

SPORTS & BEACHES

Numerous beaches line the south and east coast of the island. On the north and west coast on the other hand, there are only a few beaches, and almost all of them are only accessible by boat. The following is a selection of the best beaches, those worth a trip from other parts of the island.

BANÁNA BEACH ☘
(131 F5) (𝄞 G17)

On the Skopós Peninsula this dead straight sandy beach is over half a mile long and is still largely undeveloped. There are sun loungers under palm thatched umbrellas and sweepings views over the sea to the Peloponnese. In the eastern part there are low scrub dunes. Food and drink is served at one of the largest beach bars in Western Greece. Chill out in the hammocks or deckchairs beneath the shade of the trees. *Buses from Argássi and Zákynthos Town stop on the main road about 300 m/985 ft from the beach*

GERÁKAS BEACH ☯
(131 F5) (𝄞 G17–18)

This scenically beautiful sandy beach is where sea turtles and tourists try to coexist. Beach use is only allowed during the day and conservationists inform tourists about the correct behaviour. There are designated areas for bathing and tavernas were banned into the hinterland.

KAMÍNIA BEACH
(131 F5) (*ØØ G17*)

The about 130 m/427 ft rough sand and fine gravel beach has some Tamarisk trees that provide shade. Sun loungers and umbrellas are available on the green lawn and are even provided for free to beach bar guests. There are even some porch swings. *Buses stop on the main road about 200 m/656 ft from the beach*

MAKRÍS GIALÓS
(130 B2) (*ØØ D15*)

Well maintained gravel beach that has some sun loungers and umbrella rentals. It lies about 800 m/2624 ft south of the scenic hamlet of *Mikró Nisí*, which is built in an idyllic location on a flat ledge that protrudes into the sea.

INSIDER TIP MINIATURE GOLF
(131 E4) (*ØØ F17*)

One of the most idiosyncratic miniature golf courses in Europe is the work of one local. The two 18 hole courses include replicas of Stonehenge, the Golden Gate Bridge, the Statue of Liberty, the Irish Blarney Castle, the Leaning Tower of Pisa and many other world famous landmarks which are integral parts of the courses. In the evening, the course is attractively lit. *Daily 10am–2am | Argássi | www.world-tourminigolf.com*

MOTOR BOATS

If you rent a motor boat (no licence required) in *Límni Kerioú*, you can cross the Bay of Laganás or circle the turtle island of Marathonísi. If you decide to set sail on your own from *Ágios Nikólaos*, you can even visit the Blue Caves or the Shipwreck Beach – provided calm seas are forecast. *From 70 euros/day*

MOUNTAIN BIKING & HIKING

Bicycle rentals and guided mountain bike tours are offered by *Podilatadiko (Zákynthos Town | Platía Agíou Pávlou/ Odós Koutouzi 88 | tel. 26 95 02 44 34 | www.podilatadiko.com)*. The longest tour is 120 km/75 miles around the island, the most strenuous is a 35 km/22 mile long crossing of the island mountains. Guided hikes are also arranged. Dates and prices are subject to demand and the number of participants.

SAN NICOLAS BEACH
(131 F5) (*ØØ G17*)

A 300 m/984 ft sandy beach on Skopós Island that has sun lounger rentals, beach bar, showers and water sports activities. In the north the beach is bordered by the *Saint Nicholas chapel* on a low, rocky promontory, which is especially lovely at dusk. *Free shuttle buses in the morning from Laganás (Hotel Laganás), Kalamáki (main intersection) and Argássi (Hotel Mimósa)*

INSIDER TIP XIGIÁ BEACH
(130 C2) (*ØØ E15*)

Xigiá Beach promises an adventurous day at the beach thanks to its special cantína. Before finding a spot to sunbathe, swim inside the tiny rocky bay where the bright blue water from the cooling sulphur springs splashes against two tiny coves. This healing water is supposedly good for your complexion and, depending on the current, flows into the bay and sometimes far out to sea. Follow the signpost 2 minutes downhill to the "spa" which was once planned but never built and take a plunge in these healing waters. If you need a drink afterwards, order one from the counter on the beach and it will be wheeled down to you in a small wicker basket from the cantína at the top. An old bicycle is standing in a vertical position at the edge of the cliff and its pedals and chain are used as the pulley system *Directly on the main road around the island*

ENTERTAINMENT

INSIDER TIP 34
(131 E4) (*☐ F16–17*)

Zákynthos also has its own alternative culture scene; its meeting place is this café-bar which also serves warm snacks. The bar attracts a crowd of left-winged, alternative individuals who like to come here with their families to play cards and board games. Live music is sometimes played – but you won't hear any traditional folk music here. *Daily from 9am | Zákynthos Town | Odós Filíta 34 | Budget*

O ADELFÓS TU KÓSTA/
KOSTAS' BROTHER TAVERNA
(131 F4) (*☐ G17*)

An idyllically situated garden taverna where *kantádes* are sung in the evenings on weekends. Specialities of the house are rabbit and *kokorás ragú*, a chicken ragout with lots of vegetables. *Open during carnival, the Easter holidays and June–Sept Fri–Sun from 8pm, July/August also on other days | below the main road between Banána Beach and Ionion Beach | Moderate*

SARAKÍNA (131 D5) (*☐ F17*)

Costumed locals perform Greek dances every evening from 7pm–9pm in the large taverna next to the ruins of the historic manor of Sarakína, they also sing *kantádes*. The event even ends with a Greek party where the guests may dance along. A free minibus shuttles between

the restaurant and various stops in Laganás from 6.30–10pm. *2 km/1.2 mile from the centre of Laganás on the road to Pantokrátoras, clearly signposted | tel. 26 95 05 16 06 | Expensive*

Gerákas Beach: up close and personal with the sea turtles

VARKARÓLA ★ ●
(131 E4) (*☐ F16–17*)

You will hear Zakynthian *kantádes* every evening in this taverna on the harbour road. Often guests with their own instruments and good voices join in resulting in spontaneous international music evenings. They have a selection of snacks to eat, and to drink 🍷 they serve a dry, organically grown Verdea wine from the vineyards of host Yiannis and his brother Kóstas. *Daily from noon, music from approx. 9pm | Zákynthos Town | Odós Lomvárdou 30 | Moderate*

WHERE TO STAY

APELÁTI ⭐
(131 D6) (*⊞ E18*)

A modern house that doubles as a restaurant and affordable guesthouse on a small plateau in the south-west of the island surrounded by vineyards and olive trees. The very friendly proprietress, Mrs Dénia, rents out five modern rooms with bathrooms; the women of the family prepare good home-style cooking in the kitchen. Vegetables, wine, goat and rabbit mostly come from their own farm. *Kerí | off the main road from Límni Kerioú to Kerí | tel. 26 95 03 33 24 | Budget*

BALCONY
(131 D3) (*⊞ F16*)

Modern hotel built in the traditional *Zákynthos* style, on a promontory overlooking the Bay of Tsílivi. Steps lead you down to the sandy beach. *34 rooms | Tsíliví | 500 m/1640 ft from the village centre on the road to Zákynthos | tel. 26 95 02 61 79 | www.balconyhotel.gr | Budget*

CRYSTAL BEACH (131 E4) (*⊞ F17*)

Surrounded by old palm trees and tamarisk, this exclusive hideaway beach hotel blends perfectly into the surrounding landscape and you will be forgiven for forgetting that Laganás is close by. There is no other hotel on the beach and you will not be disturbed by the bars at Kalamáki. If you insist on the Bay of Laganás, make sure to stay here! *62 rooms | Kalamáki Beach | tel. 26 95 04 27 74 | www.crystalbeach.gr | Moderate*

INSIDER TIP ▶ DAPHNE'S STUDIOS
(131 F5) (*⊞ G17*)

Only 100 m/328 ft from Pórto Róma Beach the seven ground floor apartments and four holiday houses of Dionýsis Tsilimígras and his Swedish wife María are set in a quiet, green oasis on the edge of a forest. On the terraces of the sprawling grounds there are loungers and hammocks and the kitchens are well above average. Four mountain bikes are available for use at no additional charge. *Vassilikós | Pórto Róma | tel. 26 95 03 53 19 | www.daphnes-zakynthos. com | Moderate*

IONIAN STAR (130 C3) (*⊞ E16*)

Friendly beach hotel with roadside pool, situated directly at the estuary. Good base to explore the island's north. *25 rooms | Alikés | tel. 26 95 08 34 16 | www.ionian-star.gr | Moderate*

INSIDER TIP ▶ MÝLOS ☀
(130 B1) (*⊞ D15*)

A very romantic option with wonderful views are these two well-equipped windmill imitations on the cliff directly above the Blue Caves. There are steps leading down to a small sun terrace by the sea and there is a taverna 200 m away. *2 apartments (2–4 persons) | Cape Skinári | tel. 26 95 03 11 32, mobile tel. 69 72 05 57 11 | www.potamitisbros.gr | Expensive*

PÓRTO KOÚKLA BEACH
(131 D5) (*⊞ F18*)

Small hotel set in a green area on a long, narrow sandy beach south of the islet Ágios Sóstis, with a host who loves to sing! Turtles are not endangered on this beach. *35 rooms | Lithákia | signposted access off the Laganás-Kerí road 3 km/1.9 mile away | tel. 26 95 05 23 93 | www. porto-koukla.com.gr | Moderate*

Something unusual: holiday accommodation in a Mýlos windmill replica on Cape Skinári

STRADA MARINA ☼
(131 E4) (𝘮 F17)

If you want to stay in this lively town, the best address is the Strada Marina. Make sure to book a room with a sea view as they have large balconies from which you can enjoy the sun rise above the Peloponnese Mountains in the morning. The hotel has a rooftop pool and buses from outside the hotel shuttle passengers to the region's beaches. *112 rooms | Odós K. Lomvárdou 14 | Zákynthos Town | tel. 26 95 04 27 61 | www.stradamarina.gr | Moderate*

INFORMATION

TOURISM POLICE
(131 E4) (𝘮 F16–17)
Zákynthos Town | Odós Lombardoú 62 | tel. 26 95 02 73 67

FERRY CONNECTIONS

All year round car ferries travel several times daily between Zákynthos Town and Killíni (Peloponnese). The ferry operators are in a constant price war with each other and tickets are sometimes available for as little as 3 euros. From May until October a ferry travels twice daily between Ágios Nikólaos/Skinári and Pessáda (Kefaloniá). *Mon–Sat first ferry to Killíni 5.30am, Sun 8am, last ferry from Killíni daily 9.30pm*

WHERE TO GO

OLYMPIA ★ (0) (𝘮 0)
▓▓▓ MAP INSIDE BACK COVER
The place where the Olympic Games originated is an easy day trip. You can book it as a boat-bus tour through a travel agency or go there on your own by car. From Zákynthos to the ferry port of

Olympia: the town of ancient sports and architectural legends

Killíni takes about 90 minutes, from there it is another 75 km/47 miles on a well maintained road to Olympia.

The Olympic Games took place for more than 1100 years in the ancient Greek sanctuary of Olympia. They started in 776 BC and were held for the last time around AD 400, before they were once again revived 1500 years later in their modern form.

Tour: The best place to start your tour, if you want to understand Olympia and not just see it, is the *Temple of Zeus*. You will easily spot the temple with its three tiered base and the many massive column remains that are toppled on it and around it. This temple was the religious centre of the sanctuary. On the almost 28 m/92 ft wide and over 64 m/210 ft long upper step of the substructure there

once stood 36 Doric columns, each over 10 m/33 ft high. Completed in 457 BC, the main structure of the temple was built out of limestone and surrounded a windowless *cella*, with a doorway in the east. In its interior, in mystical semi-darkness, stood one of the seven wonders of the ancient world: a 13 m/43 ft high hollow statue of Zeus made from gold, silver, ivory and precious stones. It was the work of Phidias, who also had a hand in the creation of the adornments for the Parthenon Temple in the Athenian Acropolis. On the western opposite side of the temple are the high brick walls of a 5th century *basilica* which was built in the place where Phidias' workshop once stood.

South of the workshop there used to be the *Leonidaion*, the lodgings of the guests of honour dating from the 4th century, which was embellished in Roman times by a large, still identifiable water basin. North of the *workshop of Phidias* is the large 3rd century BC *Palaistra* with still visible rows of columns where the wrestling matches were carried out. In the northern part of the courtyard is the preserved grooved pavement that gave the wrestlers more grip and stability.

Looking north from the Temple of Zeus you will see the *Temple of Hera*, which has a number of different types of columns. Some are made from up until ten pieces of column, some of only a few pieces and their capitals are also different, one of the pillars has only 16 instead of the usual 20 flutings. This indicates that the temple (built around 600 BC) originally had wooden columns, which were replaced by stone ones over the centuries, each corresponding to the style of the time.

To the one side of the Temple of Hera is the *Nyphaeum* (a semi-circular fountain from the Roman era) with a *terrace* where an array of treasuries representing the eleven Greek city states once stood. This was where they held their most valuable votive offerings to Zeus. Numerous votive offerings of other city states were set up around the sacred precinct.

The treasuries terrace ends at the *entrance to the stadium*, originally covered by a vaulted roof. A part of it was reconstructed by archaeologists. Right at the entrance you can see the long stretch of the foundations of the *Echo Hall*, a 98 m/321 ft long lobby that provided protection from the rain and the midday sun. The ancient *Olympic stadium* is a surprisingly simple building. It could accommodate 45 000 spectators in the surrounding well-preserved mud seats.

Only the referees sat on stone benches. The stone start and finish lines can still clearly be seen at both ends of the stadium.

On the way back to the entrance of the excavation area lie the remains of the *Philippeion*: two circular foundations that once supported a round temple. The Macedonian King Philip II donated it in 338 BC, his son Alexander the Great completed it.

North of the Philippeion you can see the remains of the *Prytaneion*, where the Olympic champions were entertained. On the other side of the road lie the scant remains of the 3rd century BC *gymnasium* where the Olympians trained on an elongated space surrounded by colonnades *(April–Oct daily 8am–8pm, Nov–March 8am–6.30pm or sunset (Good Friday noon–5pm), 1 Jan, 25 March, orthodox Easter Sunday, 1 May, 25/26 Dec closed | combined ticket with Archaeological Museum 12 euros)*.

In the *Archaeological Museum* opposite the archaeological site holds some of the greatest art treasures of Greece. These include the marble sculptures from the pediment area of the Temple of Zeus and its metopes, marble panels with relief plates, a large bronze horse dating from around 800 BC, the chalice of the sculptor Phidias and a Roman statue of a bull. The two most famous statues are the Hermes of Praxiteles and Nike the goddess of victory, both works from the Classical era *(same opening times as the excavations)*.

The displays in the *Museum of the History of the Olympic Games* include ancient sporting equipment while the *Museum of the History of Excavations* show the work of archaeologists *(opening times as per the Archaeological Museum | free admission)*.

DISCOVERY TOURS

① FOUR IONIAN ISLANDS AT A GLANCE

START: ① Zákynthos Town	**11 days**
END: ㉚ Vafkéri	**Driving time**
Distance: 🚗 638 km/396 miles, 430 km/267 miles of which by car/ taxi/bus	**(without stops) 24 hours**

COSTS: Around 1200 euros per person for accommodation, food, admission fees, boat trips, activities, ferries, inland flight, hire car incl. petrol, bike hire (July/Aug the same plus 20 percent)

IMPORTANT TIPS: Zákynthos bus timetable at *www.ktel-zakynthos.gr*, flight Zákynthos – Kefaloniá: *www.skyexpress.gr*; Kefaloniá bus timetable: *www.ktelkefalonias.gr*, ferry Kefaloniá – Ithaca: *www.ionionpelagos.com*, hiring of rental cars in Ithaca: *www.agscars.com*, ferry Ithaca–Léfkas: *www.borsalinotravel.gr*

Would you like to explore the places that are unique to this region? Then the Discovery Tours are just the thing for you – they include terrific tips for stops worth making, breathtaking places to visit, selected restaurants and fun activities. It's even easier with the Touring App: download the tour with map and route to your smartphone using the QR Code on pages 2/3 or from the website address in the footer below – and you'll never get lost again even when you're offline.

TOURING APP

→ p. 2/3

If you have the time and energy for island hopping, this action-packed tour will take you to all four islands in just a little under two weeks. You do need to be flexible but don't worry, the tour will certainly not end in an odyssey. You will feel more like Phileas Fogg, who, according to his creator Jules Verne, travelled around the world in eighty days and had stories to tell of his adventures when he arrived home.

Take a taxi from the island's airport to ❶ **Zákynthos Town** → p. 74 and the hotel **Strada Marina** → p. 81. To stretch your legs after the flight, walk up to the panoramic village

DAY 1

❶ Zákynthos Town

85

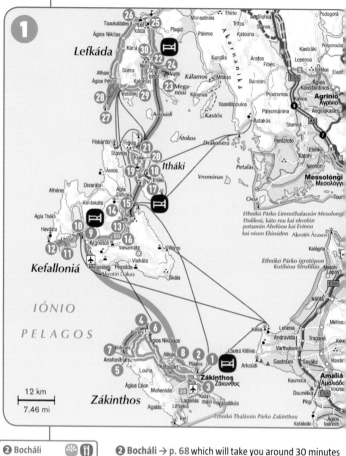

| ❷ Boch**á**li | ❄ 🍴 |

❷ Boch**á**li → p. 68 which will take you around 30 minutes and enjoy an expresso and a piece of lemon cake when you get there. In the evening, head to the taverna **Varkaróla** → p. 79 where traditional *kantádes* are sung from 9pm onwards to get you in the mood for the trip ahead.

DAY 2

9 km/5.6 miles

If you are up bright and early and manage to visit **Zákynthos Museum** → p. 74 before 10am, you will be treated to the splendid sight of the museum's icons lit up by the morning sun. After your museum visit, **wander from St. Mark's square and along the main shopping street A. Roma** where you can buy authentic Greek food in **Éllinon Géfsis** → p. 77

for a picnic later on. Your next stop is the church **Ágios Dioníssios → p. 74** situated virtually on the harbour front, from where you can **head back along the promenade to your hotel**. Deposit your purchases in your room and enjoy your picnic on the balcony with views of the Peloponnese Mountains in the background. Around 3pm, you can take your first dip in the Ionian Sea followed by a bus ride to **❸ Argássi → p. 67**. The most romantic spot for a swim is at the old English bridge in front of the **Xénos Kamára Beach** hotel where you can enjoy a coffee afterwards on the hotel's poolside terrace. The next activity is mini golf at probably one of Europe's craziest **mini golf course → p. 78** (500 m/546 yd from the Xénos Kamára Beach Hotel). Then **return to the Strada Marina** hotel **by bus or taxi.** In the evening, dine at **Alesta → p. 75** on St. Mark's square which serves the best pizzas and salads on the market.

Today it gets amphibious. Set off in your hire car at 9am at the latest and head to the **island's most northerly point at the lighthouse at Cape Skinári → p. 68.** From here you can take a small motor boat (it has to be small to enter the caves!) to the **❹ Blue Grottos → p. 68** and even bathe in the magical light inside. 20 minutes later, swap onto a larger speedboat that jets you off to the world-famous **❺ Shipwreck Beach → p. 73** where you can spend 40 minutes including a swim. You'll be back at your car around 1.30pm and will be ready for a bite to eat at **❻ Taverna Fáros** (Budget), **a two minutes' drive from Cape Skinári. Then take the road to Volimes and, on leaving the town, steer towards the coast:** Be brave and enjoy the splendid view from the **❼ Skywalk**, to the Shipwreck Beach below. The stalls in front of the skywalk sell INSIDER TIP Corinthian currants, a perfect snack for the days ahead of you. **Now drive across the island** to reach the taverna **Fioro tou Levante → p. 75** for an early evening meal. Situated on the hill with the church **❽ Áno Gerakári → p. 67**, the taverna's terrace offers splendid views not only of Zákynthos but of Kefaloniá too. A special spot for a nightcap is on one of the balconies of the **Bliss Bar** (daily from noon) in the island's capital.

Around lunch time the next day, a propeller plane will fly you at a low height in ten minutes from Zakynthos to **Kefaloniá. Then take a taxi to ❾ Argostóli → p. 40** to spend three nights at the hotel **Ionian Plaza → p. 50**, whose balconies overlook the expansive main square below. Once

❸ Argássi

DAY 3

43.5 km/27 mi

❹ Blue Grottos

12.5 km/7.8 mi

❺ Shipwreck Beach

13 km/8 mi

❻ Taverna Fáros

14.5 km/9 mi

❼ Skywalk

26 km/16mi

❽ Áno Gerakári

DAY 4

79.5 km/49 mi

❾ Argostóli

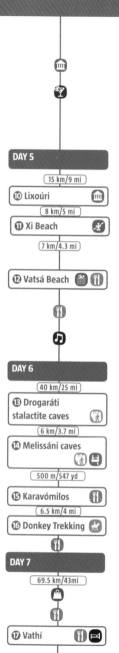

DAY 5

15 km/9 mi

⑩ Lixoúri

8 km/5 mi

⑪ Xi Beach

7 km/4.3 mi

⑫ Vatsá Beach

DAY 6

40 km/25 mi

⑬ Drogaráti stalactite caves

6 km/3.7 mi

⑭ Melissáni caves

500 m/547 yd

⑮ Karavómilos

6.5 km/4 mi

⑯ Donkey Trekking

DAY 7

69.5 km/43mi

⑰ Vathí

you have picked up your pre-booked bikes from **Aionos Bicycle Store → p. 100 cycle along the bay to the two sea water mills → p. 43**. The second of the two mill houses the café **Thalassómilos → p. 45** with young, international music and tasty cocktails, including non-alcoholic mixes. At sunset, **cycle back into town** and take a seat at one of the tables on the wooden planks outside **Kianí Aktí → p. 47** and enjoy a meal directly over the water. The seafood is a popular favourite at this tavern.

At 9.30am the next day, push your bike ontoto the ferry and soak in the views on the **20-minute crossing to ⑩ Lixoúri → p. 45**. **Follow the bike signs** to the unique **⑪ Xi Beach → p. 49** with its red sand surrounded by light grey cliffs. At the Baywatch Beach House, you can hire a canoe from **Baywatch Watersports → p. 49** to spend the next hour gliding through the waters. Then **continue by bike to ⑫ Vatsá Beach → p. 49** with its laid-back hippie atmosphere. First go for a swim and then dine at the beach's only **taverna** followed by a siesta on the beach. **You'll need 70 to 90 minutes to return to the ferry.** As a treat after all your physical exertions, go for a meal at **Paparazzi** *(daily from 7.30pm | Moderate)* and then music at the **Bass Club → p. 49**, the most famous disco on Kefaloniá.

Your day starts at 10am and you'll need a hire car to drive **across the island.** The first item on your itinerary is a descent into the **⑬ Drogaráti stalactite caves → p. 42** and then through the **⑭ Melissáni caves → p. 45** by boat. Back to daylight, enjoy a meal followed by a refreshing freddo capuccino lying in a hammock at the sea-front taverna **⑮ Karavómilos → p. 43**. The next stop is in Grizáta around 4pm where Katharina from **⑯ Donkey Trekking → p. 106** will meet you to escort you on a two-hour donkey trek. Your final meal on the island can be enjoyed at the restaurant **Captain's Table** *(Moderate)* in close proximity to your hotel.

Stop in Argostóli for a spot of shopping in the morning and treat yourself to at least one slice of cake from the **confectionery** on the main square. A **public bus running at 1pm will take you to Sámi → p. 46**, from where a ferry departs around 2.45pm to Pisoaétos on Ithaca. You should find your pre-booked hire car waiting for you at the port. **Drive to the hotel Mentor → p. 37** in the island town of **⑰ Vathí → p. 35** where you will spend two nights (remember to book in ad-

Forget yoga classes – a donkey ride is the ultimate way to relax on Greek islands

vance). For a swim late afternoon, **drive along the south side of the port bay and follow the sign to** ⑬ **Loutsá Beach**. The 20m/65ft pebbly beach is just wide enough for a plunge. Stop **on your way back** at the taverna **Kalkánis** → p. 36 for an authentic Greek meal with hearty dishes.

Today you can explore **by hire car** Odysseus' island of birth. After a brief visit inside the ⑲ **Katharón Monastery** → p. 34 and the curch of ⑳ **Anogí** → p. 33, head to ㉑ **Kióni** → p. 34, the island's prettiest village. Following lunch at the taverna **Mills** → p. 36 it's worth browsing around **Techníma** → p. 36 ranked as one of the nicest jewellers in Greece, before hiring a motor boat and playing at being your own captain. You have three hours to explore the region's tiny beaches and coves at your pleasure. **Now drive back to Vathí by car along the island's west coast** and dine in the evening at the taverna **Sirínes** → p. 36, before you soak in the views over the idyllic bay in moonlight from your balcony.

At 9am today, **a taxi takes you to Fríkes** in the island's north. **From there, take a ferry at 10.15am to** ㉒ **Nidrí** → p. 56 **on Léfkas**. The crossing takes around two hours. Your hotel for the next three nights is the **Nydrion Beach** (Budget–Moderate), **located just 5 minutes on foot from**

the ferry terminal. The hotel stands on the sea front, the perfect location for a quick swim before lunch at the portside restaurant **Pipéri** *(Moderate)*. Sport is on this afternoon's agenda. **Dennis Watersports Centre → p. 59** at the northern end of the village offers parasailing sessions for the more adventurous tourists. Two-seater kites are also available for hire. After your thrilling experience, you can relax next door in the **Sail-Inn → p. 59** beach club before returning to the port for your evening meal.

DAY 10

11 km/7mi

㉓ Meganísi

4 km/2.5 mi

㉔ Skórpios

19 km/12 mi

㉕ Lefkáda

Treat yourself to a relaxing day by the sea today. **The excursion boat from Borsalino Travel → p. 62 departs at 9.30am** and ferries you to the island of ㉓ **Meganísi → p. 62** and to the beaches on the privately-owned island of ㉔ **Skórpios → p. 63**, which once belonged to the legendary Aristotélis Onássis and now the daughter of a Russian business magnate. The crew prepares a filling BBQ on-board for guests. You return to **Nidrí around 5.30pm from where you can take the bus in the evening** to the island's capital ㉕ **Lefkáda → p. 55.** Start your evening chilling out in Caribbean style at the **Cubana Salsa Bar → p. 60** followed by an evening meal at the taverna **Lighthouse → p. 57**. If you want to party, head to **Pure → p. 60** on the promenade, which promises to be "the only club in town". **You will need to take a taxi to return to Nidri.**

DAY 11

36 km/22 mi

㉖ Faneroménis Monastery

44.5 km/27.5 mi

㉗ Cape Doukáto

9.5 km/6 mi

㉘ Pórto Katsíki Beach

24 km/15 mi

㉙ Sivóta

28 km/17 mi

㉚ Vafkéri

Start your day at 9am with a tour of the island by hire car. **Drive past the island's capital and up to the** ㉖ **Faneroménis Monastery → p. 55** with its small **animal park** and fantastic panoramic views. **Then drive down to Agios Nikitas and then up along the west coast** to the lighthouse at the most south-westerly point of ㉗ **Cape Doukáto → p. 56.** The photogenic ㉘ **Pórto Katsíki Beach → p. 56** below the steep coastline is the perfect spot for a swim. **Back on the main road,** eat and relax in splendid surroundings at the forest taverna **Oásis → p. 58. Liotrívi** café **→ p. 58** on the bay of ㉙ **Sivóta → p. 57** is a good place to enjoy a coffee and watch the yachts sailing in and out of the bay. **Return to Nidrí and drive to the waterfalls** for a quick dip in the fresh water – a change after all the sea water. **A narrow road leads uphill to the mountain village of** ㉚ **Vafkéri**, where you can spend your final evening on this trip at the authentically Greek village taverna **O Plátanos → p. 58.** Be daring and order *frigadéli,* pieces of liver in intestines – a hearty island speciality.

A DAY AMONG TURTLES ON ZÁKYNTHOS

| START: ❶ Zákynthos Town | 13 hours |
| END: ❽ Kalamáki Beach | Driving time (without stops) 2.5 hours |

Distance:
➡ 80 km/50 miles

COSTS: 65 euros per person for hire car/motorbike incl. petrol, food and kayak tour
WHAT TO PACK: Swimwear

IMPORTANT TIPS: Kayak hire: *tel. 2 695 026 626 | www.villa-nostos.com*
An alternative to a kayak is a guided boat tour from Laganás Beach, departs every hour an hour, 25 euros. The tour can also be done by motorbike or scooter.

Long before there were humans, sea turtles were laying their eggs on the sandy beaches around the Bay of Laganás. Tourism seriously threatened the existence of the loggerhead turtle but nature conservationists and tourists have now come to a good compromise. This tour brings you up close to these turtles and you can swim and sunbathe without disturbing the turtles' natural habitat. Nature conservationists are also on hand to provide interesting information on the local flora and fauna.

09:00am From ❶ **Zákynthos Town** → p. 74 **drive via Argássi to the Skopós Peninsula where the narrow and bendy road ends at** ❷ **Gerákas Beach** → p. 77. The small private exhibition at the Mediterranean Marine Life Centre informs tourists about the sea turtles and land turtles and about the nature on the land areas of the Marine National Park. The staff of the national park welcome visitors to the beach, explain how they should behave and provide up-to-date information, e.g. on the current number of turtle nests on the beach. For an early lunchtime snack, **drive back towards town** and stop for a break in the well-signposted ❸ **Banána Beach Bar** → p. 77.

01:00pm **Continue past Argássi** to the Bay of ❹ **Kalamáki** → p. 69. Here you can hire a two-seater kayak at the **Nostós X Beach Bar** and paddle along the beach close to the harbour for the next hour. INSIDER TIP Between July and September, you have a good chance of

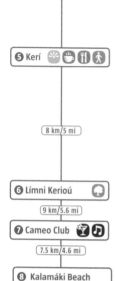

⑤ Kerí ☀ ☕ 🍴 🏃

（8 km/5 mi）

⑥ Límni Kerioú 🎧

（9 km/5.6 mi）

⑦ Cameo Club 🍸 🎵

（7.5 km/4.6 mi）

⑧ Kalamáki Beach
🍴 🎵

seeing sea turtles swimming in the water below. But don't
worry: you will not disturb the creatures by paddling in a
kayak. After your kayak tour, **cross Laganás** and drive to
the lighthouse at ⑤ Kerí → p. 69. Take a seat at the
cantína on one of the straw bales and enjoy the panoramic views along the coastline. On your way back, stop
at the taverna To Fanári tou Kerioú → p. 77 where you will
see the Greek flag flying on calmer days. A short **Skywalk**
over a glass floor offers the perfect location for fantastic
photos of the cliffs at Mizíthres – provided you are brave
enough.

`05:00pm` Don't let happiness pass you by and make sure
to visit the **Herodotus Spring** in ⑥ Límni Kerioú → p. 69.
**Then head to the port of Laganás, Porto Sostis. An adven-
turous bridge takes you on foot** to the privately owned
island of ⑦ Cameo Club (Budget), where you can relax to
the gentle music playing. The taverna Zépos → p. 77 is
waiting at ⑧ Kalamáki Beach → p. 69 to welcome guests
in the evening and is ranked as one of the best on the island.
With a little luck (which you have hopefully taken with you
from Herodotus Spring), you can dine accompanied by live
Greek music.

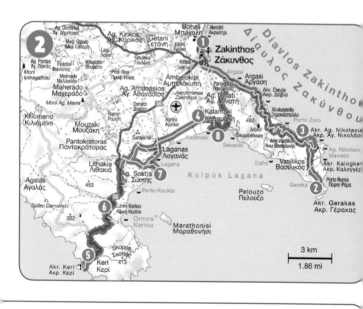

3 ITHACA – IN THE FOOTSTEPS OF ODYSSEUS

START: ① Vathí	1 day
END: ① Vathí	Walking time (without stops)
Distance: easy	9 hours
🚗 30 km/18 miles · ·⬛ Height: 300 m/980 ft	

COSTS: 55 euros per person for boat hire including petrol, lunch and evening meal

WHAT TO PACK: swimwear, shoes with sturdy soles, torch, snacks

IMPORTANT TIPS: Boat hire: *tel. 6 940 035 670 | www.rent aboatithaca.com*
It is better not to drink the water from the ⑥ Arethoúsa Spring
The Odyssey is available free online. A List of English translations can be found at *en.wikipedia.org/wiki/English_translations_of_Homer*

If not an odyssey, this tour takes you in the footsteps of the Homeric epic, guaranteeing an eventful day. The island's wild natural beauty alone promises tranquillity and solitude. You need to be in average physical condition to tackle this walk. That said King Odyssey only had a boat and his own two feet!

`09:30am` Like elsewhere in Greece, you do not need a licence or previous experience to hire a motor boat on the island. From ① Vathí → p. 35, **drive to** ② Dexiá Bay → p. 34, where Odysseus first set foot on the island laden with treasure after his ten-year epic journey. Luckily, your baggage is somewhat lighter for the **1.5-hour hike up to the** ③ Grotto of the Nymphs → p. 35, where Odysseus once hid his treasures. After this demanding walk, enjoy a refreshing swim at ④ Dexiá Beach, before you spend a little time `INSIDER TIP` cruising around the Bay of Vathí.

`01:30pm` Once you have returned the motor boat, it's time for a bite to eat in ⑤ Vathí at the market taverna Trechantíri → p. 36, where food is freshly cooked every day. Your second hike of the day now starts **at the promenade where you will see a signpost "9 Anemodouri–Arethousa Krini" shortly before the Hotel Méntor.** Follow this sign out of town along the well-paved road where you will see another sign to the ⑥ Arethoúsa Spring → p. 34 **which takes**

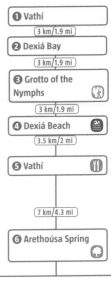

① Vathí
3 km/1.9 mi
② Dexiá Bay
3 km/1.9 mi
③ Grotto of the Nymphs
3 km/1.9 mi
④ Dexiá Beach
3.5 km/2 mi
⑤ Vathí
7 km/4.3 mi
⑥ Arethoúsa Spring

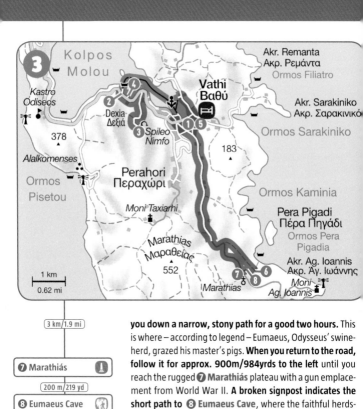

| 3 km/1.9 mi |

you down a narrow, stony path for a good two hours. This is where – according to legend – Eumaeus, Odysseus' swineherd, grazed his master's pigs. **When you return to the road, follow it for approx. 900m/984yrds to the left** until you reach the rugged **7 Marathiás** plateau with a gun emplacement from World War II. **A broken signpost indicates the short path to 8 Eumaeus Cave**, where the faithful herdsman supposedly once lived.

| 7 Marathiás | 1 |
| 200 m/219 yd |
| 8 Eumaeus Cave | 🚶 |
| 7 km/4.3 mi |

The Bay of Vathí - drop your anchor offshore and soak in the amazing views

05:00pm To return, you need to **backtrack for approx. 90 minutes** to ① Vathí → p. 35 and your room with sea view at the Hotel **Méntor** → p. 37. You can stock up at the **supermarket** next door to the hotel on cheese, olives, fruit and tomatoes to enjoy the rest of your evening on your balcony accompanied by a bottle of wine (and maybe a copy of the Odyssey...).

4 KEFALONIÁ'S BEAUTIFUL NORTH

START: ① Argostóli	1 day
END: ① Argostóli	Driving time
Distance:	(without stops)
⟷ 138 km/86 miles	4 hours

COSTS: 50 euros per person for hire car/motorbike including petrol, lunch and evening meal
WHAT TO PACK: swimwear, water shoes if needed

IMPORTANT TIPS: The tour can also be done by motorbike.

There are only two seaside villages in the north of Kefaloniá: Ássos and Fiskárdo: both are among the prettiest resorts in the Ionian Sea where you can sunbathe and swim. The northern coast is also home to Mírtos Beach, a popular film location for Hollywood stars. This tour includes two short walks, freshly brewed herbal tea in a mountain village café and you are sure to encounter herds of sheep and goats on the winding mountain roads. Try feeding them grass or hay through your car window!

09:00am The route from ① Argostóli → p. 40 to Ássos and Fiskárdo along the hillsides is well signposted and your first stop is Divaráta. The direct road from Divaráta to ② Ássos → p. 41 collapsed during the earthquake in 2011. **The diversion is signposted and takes you over the Kaló Óros plateau.** Leave your car at the car park and **follow the 25-minute trail up to the Venetian Castle.** Afterwards, take a dip at the village's tiny beach before enjoying a bite to eat at the **Plátanos** (*Budget*) taverna on the village square where the specialities include goat kid or different island cheeses.

01:00pm Now continue through the mountains to ③ Fiskárdo → p. 42 in the far north. **Follow the sign to the ferry** and park up at the end of the road behind the Nicolas taverna. **A signposted INSIDERTIP loop trail takes**

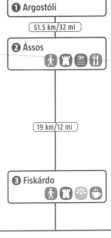

① Argostóli
51.5 km/32 mi
② Ássos
19 km/12 mi
③ Fiskárdo

you to the small **lighthouse** and to the ruins of a **Gothic church**. You'll be back at your car after approx. 40 minutes and will have time to stroll along the resort's **promenade** drink a coffee and see the yachts.

04:00pm Continue through Mesovouniá inland up to the mountain village of ④ **Kariá**. 🌀 **Rosie's Kitchen Bar →** p. 48 will welcome you with a freshly made thyme or Melissa herbal tea. There is no better place to purchase the island's herbs to take home as a souvenir. After this revitalising brew, **take the road over the east coast towards Agía Efímia to Xiropótamos and then follow the signs to Divaráta. From here, a winding road leads you down the cliffs to** ⑤ **Mírtos Beach →** p. 49 – one of the most popular postcard beaches in Greece. Visitors to the beach include the actors Penelope Cruz and Nicholas Cage for the filming of "Captain Corelli's Mandolin" in 2001. Drive back to ① **Argostóli →** p. 40 an hour before sunset to enjoy the last light of day – driving by night is no fun on Kefaloniá

④ Kariá 🍽️ 🛍️

19 km / 12 mi

⑤ Mírtos Beach 🏖️

30 km / 18.5 mi

① Argostóli 🍴

Fiskardo: idyllic island paradise

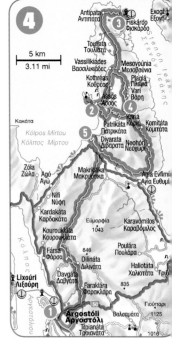

due to the state of the roads. Once you have arrived, head to the traditional mezedopolío **Beverínos**→ p. 47 for a bite to eat.

5 LÉFKAS – NESTLED BETWEEN BEACH AND MOUNTAINS

START: ❶ Lefkáda	12 hours
END: ❼ Milos Beach Club	Driving time
Distance:	(without stops)
🚗 53 km/32miles	3 hours

COSTS: 110 euros per person for hire car/motorbike including petrol, picnic, evening meal and activities (crazy sofa 20 euros, horse trek 20 euros an hour)

WHAT TO PACK: swimwear, jeans for horse trekking

IMPORTANT TIPS: pre-book horse trekking at ❻ **Aramis Farm** (also suitable for beginners) the evening before at the latest: *mobile tel. 6 938 816 164.* The tour can also be done by motorbike.

Most tourists come to the island of Léfkas for the sun, sea and sand. Those with more time on their hands drive into the mountains which climb up to heights over 1100m/3610ft. Here, you can enjoy a quiet hour on a shady village square, a picnic after a short walk in a solitary monastery ruins, a ride on horseback through green agricultural land and a swim by moonlight with views of the townscape by night.

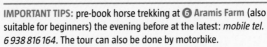

09:30am From the south end of the island's largest town ❶ **Lefkáda** → p. 55, **a road ascends to the largest of the island's mountain villages**, ❷ **Kariá** → p. 54. Two small, quirky **private museums** welcome every visitor. The **folklore museum** shows how people once lived on the island while the other exhibits old record players and radio appliances. In fact, the people who guide you around the museums are more interesting than the exhibited artefacts. Afterwards, take a seat on the large, shady **village square** underneath the old sycamore trees and watch village life pass you by. Some village inhabitants still collect water from the pretty **village well**. The village **souvenir shops** also sell local woven products – maybe a souvenir idea for your grandmother? You should definitely buy some fruit and cheese from the **general store** situated

❶ Lefkáda

12.5 km/7.8 mi

❷ Kariá

7.5 km/4.6 mi

5

2 km
1.24 mi

Akr. Girapetra
Ακρ. Γυραπέτρα
Ormos
Fleva (Varko)

Ag. Marina
Αγ. Μαρίνα ⑦
Panagia Vlaherna

Ag. Mavra
Άγ. Μαύρα Frourio
Lefkada
Λευκάδα

Lam
Λαμ
39

Akr. Ag. Ioannis
Ακρ. Αγ. Ιωάννης

Ag. Ioannis

Tsoukalades
Τσουκαλάδες

Moni
Faneromenis ⑥

Erini
Φρύνη ①

Aliki
Roleos

Peratia
Περατιά

Paralia
Pefkoulia

376

Apolpena
Απόλπενα

Arhea
Nerikos

Kaligoni
Καλήγωνη

Ag. Georgios

Kariotes
Καριότες

Ormos
Ag. Nikita

Ag. Nikitas
Άγ. Νικήτας

Kavallos
Κάβαλλος

Pal. Kariotes
Παλ. Καριότες

Ligia
Λιγιά

Nea Plagia
Νέα Πλαγ

Asprogerakata
Ασπρογερακάτα

Spanohori
Σπανοχώρι

Tembeli
Τεμπέλη

212

Drimonas
Δριμώνας

Lazarata
Λαζαράτα

Pinakohori
Πινακοχώρι

Katouna
Κατούνα

Paradisos
Παράδεισος

Pigadisani
Πηγαδισάνη

Moni Ag. Ioannou

Episkopos
Επίσκοπος

Exanthia
Εξάνθεια

Karia
Καριά ②

Alexandros
Αλέξανδρος

1040

Nikiana
Νικιάνα

Ag. Sotira

Ag. Georgios

Platistoma
Πλατύστομα

Kollivata
Κολλιβάτα

Magemenou
Μαγεμένου

Egklouvi
Εγγλούβι

Pr. Ilias

Moni Ag. Georgiou

Keramidaki
Κεραμιδάκη

Ag.
Konstantinos

Vafkeri
Βαφκέρη

Kokkini Ekklisia

652

Perigialli
Περιγιάλλι

Pasa
Πάσα

Hortata
Χορτάτα

Ag.
Donatos

Ag. Nikolaos

③

616

Moni Ag.
Asomaton ④

Pahi
Πάχη

Nidri
Νύδρι

Sparti
Σπάρτη

918

Ag. Sotiras

Margariti
Μαργαρίτη

Koloni
Κολώνι

Madouri
Μαδούρι

Ag. Theodori
Αγ. Θεόδωροι

Oros
Όρος

Elati
Ελάτη

1158

Neohori
Νεοχώρι

Ag. Kiriaki

Skorpio
Σκορπιό

1182

Ormos Drepanou

directly above the square for your picnic later on in the day. Continue your drive to **Vafkéri and in a left-hand bend just before reaching the village,** you will pass an old ③ INSIDER TIP **well** under large sycamore trees. It also has a traditional wash place and a large basin where grapes were once traditionally crushed by feet. The next item on your agenda is a stroll through the forest: **follow a small brown signpost along a narrow paved road to** ④ **Moní Asómaton → p. 56**, the ruins of a Venetian Monastery of the Archangel. Here you can enjoy your picnic in these silent surroundings and lie back on the grass to watch the skies. It's no wonder that the monks

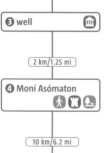

③ well 🏛

2 km/1.25 mi

④ Moní Asómaton
🚶 🏠 ⚱

10 km/6.2 mi

who once lived felt extremely close to the heavens above.

`02:30pm` **Now drive through the village of Vafkéri down to ⑤ Nidrí → p. 56**. The views of the seas with the multitude of tiny bays, hundreds of yachts, tiny privately-owned islands and the high mainland mountains are simply breathtaking. Then it's time to ride the "crazy sofa", pulled at hair-raising speeds over the water by a motor boat and organised by the **Dennis Watersports Centre → p. 59** – there is no time for a nap on this sofa! Now swap your armchair for a saddle and head to **⑥ Aramis Farm in Apolpéna on the outskirts of Léfkada.** If you book in advance, the Swedish owner Janet Nikolési-Berglund will have everything well prepared for you to enjoy a two-hour trek on horseback.

`08:00pm` Time for evening meal at the **⑦ Milos Beach Club** (*Budget*) on the spit of land to the north of the town. Its bar and taverna are the main meeting places for keen windsurfers and kite surfers and parties are often held here. If things hot up, the sea is just a stone's throw away to cool down.

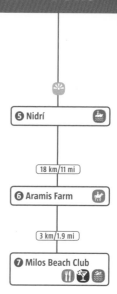

⑤ Nidrí

18 km/11 mi

⑥ Aramis Farm

3 km/1.9 mi

⑦ Milos Beach Club

Traditional mountain village life on the square in Kariá

SPORTS & ACTIVITIES

The islands are a paradise for surfers, snorkelers and divers. Yet they also offer the right terrain for mountain bikers and hikers. Although nobody comes especially for a wellness retreat, the region does have its fair share of spa and beauty facilities.

CYCLING

Kefaloniá and Léfkas are ideal for ambitious mountain bikers; one can still find several tracks in the mountains that have, at the most, only been explored by a few Jeeps. But don't underestimate the ascents!

On Kefaloniá you can get a bike and good tips at *Aionos Bicycle Store (Odós Sitempóron 61–63 | Argostóli | tel. 26 71 02 68 74 | www.ainosbicycles.gr)*. They also rent out good child seats and even bicycle trailers.

On Léfkas, *Get active (no office, contact by e-mail or mobile tel. 69 89 45 64 45 | www.getactivelefkas.com)* offers daily mountain bike guided tours of different lengths and difficulty levels. Road bikes are also available for hire. All resorts on Zákynthos also have places to hire bikes and basic mountain bikes.

From biking to windsurfing: the best places for your favourite sport and where you can also find out as much information in advance

DIVING

The ideal spot for divers is the ⭐ coast pitted with caves along the peninsula in the south-west of Límni Kerioú on Zákynthos. There are ● two very good dive centres with a lot of experience: *Turtle Beach Diving Centre, Timothéos Marmíris (Limní Kerioú | harbour | tel. 26 95 04 87 68 | www.diving-center-turtle-* beach.com)* and the *Neró Sport Diving Center (Peter & Dennis Mohr | Límni Kerioú, west of the harbour | tel. 26 95 02 84 81)*, operating all year round.

A good diving school on Léfkas is the *Léfkas Diving Center* in Nikianá *(tel. 26 45 07 21 05 | www.lefkasdivingcenter. gr)*. Another diving centre is located on the beach in Vassilikí on Léfkas: *Nautilus | mobile tel. 69 36 18 17 75 | www.underwater.gr.*

Large yachts as well as small kayaks at Fiskárdo port on Kefaloniá

FISHING

Fishing is allowed on the islands and you don't even need a licence. The professional fisherman Dimítrios, who lives in Kateliós on Kefaloniá, takes guests on fishing cruises *(Káto Kateliós | mobile tel. 69 47 66 75 95 | www.fishingtourismke falonia.com)*. The tour departs from Kateliós at 7am and returns at 2pm. Under the shade of the boat, he prepares a barbecue for lunch made of the fish caught in the nets during the morning.

HORSEBACK RIDING

For riding enthusiasts there are some INSIDER TIP excellent stables at Zerváta on Kefaloniá. Owner Cornelia Schimpfky stables the sure-footed Haflingers and offers rides – from several hours to multi-day – as well as lessons in jumping and dressage *(tel. 26 74 02 31 43, mobile tel. 69 77 53 32 03 | www.kephalonia.com/ English/Welcome.html)*.

On Zákynthos the horse-crazy Tsouráki family has more than 50 ponies and horses for beginners and experienced riders alike. They are environmentally conscious and as such do not offer ☺ beach rides, only cross-country rides *(daily from 7am | well signposted off the Argássi–Kalamáki road | free shuttle service to hotel | mobile tel. 69 77 87 57 92 | www.laganahorseriding.gr)*.

HIKING

When hiking you should always wear long pants due to the thorny undergrowth and good footwear is also essential. There are no accurate hiking maps, a few marked trails only on Kefaloniá (especially near Fiskárdo and around the Énos) and Ithaca.

SAILING

Sailing opportunities are available from Vounáki on the mainland opposite Léfkas.

The cruises take one or two weeks and even offer the beginner the opportunity to sail the area alone, as the experienced crew ensure safety from an accompanying boat. Organiser: *Sunsail (www.sunsail.co.uk)*. There are also sailing opportunities with *Skorpios-Charter (tel. 26 45 09 22 81 | www.skorpioscharter.com)*.

SEA KAYAKING

INSIDER TIP *Seakayaking Kefaloniá* offer a unique experience in Greece. The small company, run by the Swiss-Greek couple Yvonne and Pávlos, offer more than ten different day trips (each trip 60 euros) along the coast of Kefaloniá. Ideal for all ages and also for beginners. Also eight to nine day kayak tours to, among others, Léfkas, Meganísi, Kastós, Kálamos and Ithaca. *(Trapesáki | mobile tel. 69 34 01 04 00 | www.seakayakingkefalonia-greece.com)*. Guided sea kayak day trips are possible even from only two participants from Nidrí *(Info: www.trekking.gr/outdoor-holidays-in-greece/destination/ionian-sea/full-day-sea-kayak-lefkada | booking at Borsalino Travel, see p. 62)*

WATER SPORTS

With the exception of Ithaca, there are water sport centres (usually right in front of the large hotels) on all of the islands, where you can rent pedal boats, go waterskiing and kitesurfing. Motor boat rentals are big business on all four islands and anyone above 18 years old can hire 30 HP motor boats without a boat licence or previous experience. After a short briefing, you can set sail for beaches and islands which would be otherwise inaccessible. All boats are equipped with an emergency kit in case you should get into

trouble. Another popular excursion is to sail out to sea, drop anchor and then take a plunge in the open waters. The cost of daily hire depends on the horse power you choose and the season, varying between 60 – 120 euros a day. You can find operators in nearly every resort and at every port.

WELLNESS

There are only a handful of hotels on the four islands which have spa facilities. The exclusive spa at the ● *Emelisse Art Hotel (www.emelissehotel.com)* in the north of Kefaloniá promises the ultimate wellness experience. Zákynthos offers the largest selection with *Hotel Lesante (www.lesante.gr)*, *Majestic (www.hotelmajesticspa.gr)* and *Azure Resort (www.azureresort.com)* all providing wellness and spa facilities. They are also open to non-hotel guests by prior appointment.

● Vassilikí and Giórgos Balí on Kefaloniá *(Karavádos | 60 euros per person including wine and recipe book | tel. 26 71 06 94 53 | www.chezvassiliki.gr)* offer a different type of wellness program. Three times a week, they organize group cooking classes, inviting participants into their own garden to pick what they need to create a healthy meal. The groups are kept small to ensure a relaxing, authentic atmosphere and the dishes are served up as a Greek banquet.

WINDSURFING

On Léfkas many beaches have windsurfing centres. Some of the good ones are *Club Vassiliki Active Holidays (on Vassilikí beach | tel. 26 45 03 15 88 | www.clubvass.com)* and the *Mílos Windsurf Club (in the very windy region of Ágios Ioánnis near Lefkáda | mobile tel. 69 73 75 83 76 | www.milosbeach.gr)*.

TRAVEL WITH KIDS

Ithaca, Kefaloniá, Léfkas and Zákynthos are relatively small islands with relatively few permanent residents. That is why it is not viable to set up amusement parks, zoos and water parks for the locals.

There is absolutely no mass tourism on Ithaca and Kefaloniá, and on Léfkas it is still in its infancy. That is why no major investments of this kind have been made even for the tourists. There are a few modest developments on Zákynthos.

The lack of these kinds of facilities, which seem essential to us for a family holiday, lies in the fact that the Greeks are very child friendly – they just let their children take part in almost everything that older persons do – until well after midnight. Children are welcome guests at night in café bars and tavernas; they can romp around in public places, between the locals out for a stroll and even play soccer in front of the church. With many of the sporting facilities and water activities there are no set age limits so whatever the children are able to do (and what their parents allow them to do) is available for them to try.

The good weather, wonderful beaches and sea all mean that children are seldom bored. All the islands (except Ithaca) have more than enough shallow, sheltered bays where little ones can splash and swim. Almost all of the large hotels on Zákynthos also have paddling pools.

Boat trips are always great adventures and if you are experienced enough, then

Lots of fun for children and parents: the best ideas for some adventures in the water, on the sea and on land

you can even INSIDER TIP rent a motor boat and the children will love being sailors and cabin crew.

Walks here are fun even for children who are reluctant to walk with their parents at home. On the Greek Islands there are no boring and crowded trails; instead the routes are mostly used by shepherds or goat paths. Along the way there are countless lizards and sometimes you can even spot snakes. There are seldom any "do not" signs so the children can scramble around as and where as they wish –

even in the ruins and medieval castles that are almost never secured!

There are doctors who are familiar with all the usual childhood diseases, on all of the islands. Greek doctors prescribe antibiotics very readily, even for minor illnesses. So if you are critical about the overuse of antibiotics then it is best that you also pack your home remedies.

Child discounts are offered on public buses, on domestic flights, on ships and excursion boats as well as on many of the excursions for children under 12 years old. Visits to the state museums and archaeological sites are free of charge for children.

Since there are no attractions specifically aimed at children on the other islands, the following recommendations are limited to Kefaloniá and Zákynthos.

KEFALONIÁ

ARK (128 B2) (*∭ B12*)

At the animal sanctuary on Kefaloniá, over 300 gentle dogs and cats are waiting to be stroked by tourists and families who may also bring a few titbits to share among the creatures. Visitors are invited to walk around the sanctuary and play with the animals – and the voluntary helpers are pleased to receive a small donation at the end of your visit. *Daily | Argostóli | first follow the signpost to Cephalonia Botanica and at the police station follow the sign to the ARK animal rescue centre*

DONKEY RIDES ⭐

(127 E6) (*∭ D11*)

Originating from Germany, Katharina Fehring now lives on a farm near Sámi and offers treks off the beaten track in the surrounding area with her five donkeys. The donkeys can carry all your supplies and if you weigh less than 55 kg/8 stones, you can enjoy a ride on these loving grey animals. The treks last between one and eight hours. *Grizáta 1 |1st donkey 25 euros, 2nd donkey 20 euros, every further donkey 15 euros an hour | mobile tel. 69 80 05 96 30 | www.donkeytrekkingkefalonia.com*

KARAVÓMILOS ●

(127 D5) (*∭ C–D11*)

Families with children can spend an enjoyable half a day at Karavómilos Lake. The large taverna offers hammocks and deckchairs for guests to relax and enjoy the surroundings. The narrow pebble beach is suitable for children as the water remains shallow until quite far out and the lake is surrounded by shady trees. Swings hang from the trees, goats graze on the car park and ducks are waiting on the lake to be fed. A paved, shady path encircles the lake for the family to walk around and stroke the cats that cross their path – and there is even a free WiFi connection if the kids still want to play their computer games.

MINIATURE TRAIN ON WHEELS

(128 B2) (*∭ B11–12*)

Miniature trains with locomotives and three wagons, each with space for about 20 people, are popular throughout Greece. They are driven by electric motors and have rubber wheels. *Argostóli* has one that runs through the town. *Departure from the harbour, daily 8.30am–10.30pm | trip 6 euros, children 4 euros*

PLAY CHAUFFEUR

(128 B2) (*∭ B12*)

In good weather small electric jeeps or VW beetles are available daily in Argostóli in the *Luna Park* fun fair at the northern end of Odós Rizospáston *(5 euros for 15 minutes)*. The park also has remote controlled boats, table soccer and other games that delight the little ones.

ZÁKYNTHOS

ÁSKOS STONEPARK

(130 B2) (*∭ D15*)

The *Áskos Stonepark* is scenically situated between some hills in the north of the island. The park has sheep and goats, rabbits, tortoises, birds of prey and peacocks, lizards, donkeys and ponies, raccoons and many more animals. There are also ancient cisterns, cottages, stables as well as a stone wine press. The admission price is, however, disproportionate for this park, which is still under construction. *May–Sept daily 9am–7pm, Oct–April daily 10am–5pm | admission 8.50 euros, children (5–12 years) 5 euros | Áskos | www.askosstonepark.gr*

HORSE-DRAWN CARRIAGE RIDE ●
(131 E4) (*M F16–17*)

In the late afternoon horse-drawn carriages line the *Ágios Nikólaos pier* at the edge of the Platía Solomoú in Zákynthos Town. Trips through the island capital take 20 minutes and if the little ones feel brave enough then they are often also allowed to hold the reins and may sit next to the driver. Carriages are also available in *Alikés,* where they usually wait for customers on the road that runs parallel to the beach. *25 euros for 20 minute trips*

MINIATURE TRAIN ON WHEELS
(131 E4) (*M F16–17*)

Zákynthos has two miniature trains on wheels: one travels from Alikés to Pigadákia (see p. 72) while the second one goes between Argássi and the island capital. Departure in *Argássi* at the *Hotel Mimóza* on the main thoroughfare, in *Zákynthos Town* at *Platía Solomoú. Times depend on the season, but usually daily 10am–1pm and 5pm–10pm | trip 6 euros, children 4 euros*

PLAY CHAUFFEUR
(131 E4) (*M F16–17*)

On Zákynthos there are also small electric cars for children. In **INSIDER TIP** good weather daily from 6pm on the *Platía Solomoú* in Zákynthos Town, and they sometimes operate until well after 10pm. The only requirement: little ones should already be able to hold a steering wheel and to step on the pedal – which is often easier than taking their foot off the pedal. The cars have space for two children or one child and a parent (very lightweight) who wants to ride along. Parents need to keep an eye on their

Inquisitive goat at Áskos Stonepark

children as the area is not fenced. Runaways could drive anywhere from here – for as long as their batteries last. *3 euros for 10 minutes*

FESTIVALS & EVENTS

On the southern Ionian Islands many religious festivals are celebrated with traditional music, dancing and good food. Local communities and associations ensure that island culture is not neglected even during the summer. Festivals are not only organised for tourists, but also give the many Greek visitors a taste of the culture of the respective island.

The most important festival of the year is Easter. Like many other movable religious festivals, this date is set according to the Julian calendar. This is why Easter can take place up to five weeks later than elsewhere.

FEBRUARY/MARCH

Carnival Sunday: Carnival processions in all of the islands' capitals. The best one is the one in Zákynthos Town

APRIL–JUNE

Good Friday: in the morning the symbolic grave of Christ is decorated with flowers in all the churches. Evening processions in all the towns and villages

Easter Saturday: Easter mass from 11pm, which almost all Greeks attend. Shortly before midnight all the lights are turned off in the churches. At midnight the priest announces the resurrection of Christ. The worshippers light candles and the young people light noisy fireworks

Easter Sunday: Lamb and kid on the spit make up the festive meal in the gardens everywhere on the islands (a delicious smell); after lunch everyone celebrates with their family

Easter Monday: Large church festival in Kerí on Zákynthos

National holiday (unification of the Ionian Islands: the unification of the Ionian islands with Greece is celebrated in all the capitals with festivals. *21st May*

Pentecost Monday: church festival in Macherádo on Zákynthos

JULY–SEPTEMBER

Cultural summer in Argostóli on Kefaloniá and in the villages in the region with theatre performances, concerts of all kinds and folk performances. *Early July– 25 August*

Church festival in Nidrí on Léfkas. *7 July*

Wine festival on a Sunday in Ágios Ilías on Léfkas. *Second half of July*

Church festival in Exógi in the north of Ithaca with music and dance. *17 July*
Church festival in Kióni on Ithaca with music, dance and lamb on the spit. *20 July*
Church festival in Pigadákia on Zákynthos. *27 July*
One evening in August in the mountain village Kariá on Léfkas a tradition-al INSIDER TIP *Lefkadian wedding* is recre-ated and then celebrated on the village square just like in the old days. *Early August*
Large *church festival* in Stavrós on Ithaca. *5/6 August*
The largest *church festival* of the summer is celebrated in many villages, such as in Vassilikí on Léfkas and in Lixoúri on Kefaloniá. *15 August*
Week-long *International Folklore Festival* on Léfkas with participants from more than 20 countries. *Second half of August*
The large *festival of St Dioníssios, patron saint of the Ionian islands,* in Zákynthos Town is attended by many Greeks from the mainland. From about 7pm proces-sion with fireworks, afterwards festival in the streets and in the tavernas. *24 August*
On the evening of 6 September *church service and festival* at the Monastery of Katharón on Ithaca, on the next morning *icon procession* with orchestral accompa-niment. *6/7 September*

NATIONAL HOLIDAYS

1 January	New Year
6 January	Epiphany
11 March 2019, 2 March 2020	Shrove Monday
25 March	National holiday
26 April 2019, 17 April 2020	Good Friday
28/29 April 2019, 19/20 April 2020	Easter
1 May	Labour Day
21 May	Unification of the Ionian islands
16/17 June 2019, 7/8 June 2020	Whitsun
15 August	Assumption
28 October	National holiday (Ochi day)
25/26 December	Christmas

LINKS, BLOGS, APPS & MORE

www.culture.gr Official website of the Greek Ministry of Culture with lots of information and pictures of archaeological sites and museums in Greece, unfortunately not always up to date

www.ekathimerini.com Daily English language newspaper that provides a comprehensive summary of the main political, business, social and cultural news in Greece

www.visitgreece.gr/en/greek_islands/ionian_islands/zakynthos A website with information on the island's history, culture and beaches.

www.facebook.com/#!/pages/Greek-Islands/101480387302 The ideal community where you can view photos of others and post your own impressions of the Ionian Islands on an international platform

www.ecozante.com//blog#blog Diverse English-language blog which includes lots of photos. Aimed at an ecologically-minded audience

www.travelblog.org International blog mainly in English containing around 360 blogs on Zákynthos and its neighbouring islands

www.ionian-islands.com Official tourism website of the Ionian islands prefecture with information, photos, videos and the possibility of booking accomodation

www.livinginzante.com A comprehensive site set up for expats wanting to live in Zákynthos, with lots of very useful links for tourists about the various services on the island

Regardless of whether you are still researching your trip or already on the Ionian Islands: these addresses will provide you with more information, videos and networks to make your holiday even more enjoyable

vimeo.com/tag:lefkada More than 270 videos on the island of Léfkas, its beaches and activities to ensure you have an enjoyable stay on the island

www.greeka.com/ionian/kefalonia/ kefalonia-videos-1.htm Around 50 videos showing lots of different aspects of the island of Kefaloniá

www.facebook.com/virtualzakynthos. gr#!/virtualzakynthos.gr Get a glimpse into the nightlife on Zákynthos largely dominated by British and Eastern European tourists in this multilingual community

www.greeka.com/ionian/zakynthos/zakynthos-videos-1.htm A nice selection of around 30 videos in different languages about the island of Zákynthos

www.e-radio.gr Live streams of about 140 Greek radio stations, the list is sorted according to musical styles

iZante *and* iKefalonia Two free apps with a lot of general and current information on the islands of Zákynthos and Kefaloniá, 100 per cent usable offline

Lefkada Guide Free app for the island of Léfkas

Marine Traffic is a popular online service (paid app) for tracking the vessels that are passing by. The vessel's name allows you to see where it comes from, where it is headed to and other data about the ship, the flag, etc. Also handy for tracking the local ferries for which you might be waiting

Jourist Travel Interpreter is an inexpensive app that is tailored to the translation needs of tourists. The audio translations are helpful and entertaining and are accompanied by some funny illustrations

iSlands Island hoppers and excursion enthusiasts can get their timetables directly onto their phone with this free app. The search is made easier by pre-entered harbour names in English and Greek

TRAVEL TIPS

✈ During the summer there are several flights to Zákynthos. Only a few chartered flights go to Préveza/Léfkas and to Kefaloniá. There are regular flights to Zákynthos, Kefaloniá and Léfkas all year round from Athens. Enough taxis are available at all airports, there are no airport buses. You can only get to Ithaca by boat, the best way is from Killíni/Peloponnese or Kefaloniá.

Flights in the turbo-props of the Cretan airline *Sky Express (www.skyexpress.gr)* are state-subsidised, making them very affordable: Préveza to Kefaloniá (55 euros), to Zákynthos (60 euros), and between Kefaloniá and Zákynthos (56 euros). Because they fly at low altitudes, these flights are also recommended for day trippers! Even Kíthira off the south coast of the Peloponnese (historically part of the Ionian Islands) and Corfu, the main island of the archipelago, are accessible from Zákynthos, Kefaloniá and Préveza.

🚢 Car ferries connect Igoumenítsa on the mainland (for Léfkas) and Pátras on the Peloponnese (for the remaining islands) throughout the year with the Italian ports of Ancona, Brindisi and Bari. A car ferry departs for Kefaloniá from Brindisi six to eight times in July and August. *Info: Ventouris Ferries | tel. 2104 82 80 01 | ventourisferries.com*

BUSES

There are public buses on all the Ionian Islands. The fares are low and tickets are sold by the conductor in the bus. Timetable copies are available at the bus terminals of the respective islands. The timetables change several times a year depending on the season. The buses run less frequently on Saturdays and Sundays.

CAMPING

Camping anywhere else than in a camp site is prohibited but is often done on isolated beaches. Many of the islands have official campsites which are usually only open between May and September.

CAR HIRE

Mopeds, scooters, motorbikes and cars are available for rent on virtually all the islands. However, mopeds and motorcycles are often in a bad condition and unexperienced drivers are the cause of many accidents. Rental cars are offered by many companies. To rent a car you must be over 21; the national driving li-

RESPONSIBLE TRAVEL

It doesn't take a lot to be environmentally friendly whilst travelling. Don't just think about your carbon footprint whilst flying to and from your holiday destination but also about how you can protect nature and culture abroad. As a tourist it is especially important to respect nature, look out for local products, cycle instead of driving, save water and much more. If you would like to find out more about eco-tourism please visit: *www.ecotourism.org*

cence is sufficient. A small car like a Vauxhall Corsa will cost about 25 euros per day including mileage, full comprehensive cover and tax.

Caution: damage to the tyres and on the underside of the car is usually not covered by insurance.

CONSULATES & EMBASSIES

UK EMBASSY
1 Ploutarchou Street | 10675 Athens | tel. 2107272600 | www.gov.uk/world/organisations/british-embassy-athens

UK CONSULATE
28 Foskolou Street | 29100 Zákynthos | tel. 2695022906| www.gov.uk/world/organisations/british-honorary-vice-consulate-zakynthos

US EMBASSY
91 Vasilissis Sophias Avenue | Athens | tel. 2107212951 | gr.usembassy.gov

CANADIAN EMBASSY
48 Ethnikis Antistaseos Street | 15231 Athens | tel. 210-72 73 400 | international.gc.ca/world-monde/greece-grece/athens-athenes.aspx?lang=eng

CUSTOMS

For EU citizens the following duty free allowances apply (import and export): for own consumption 800 cigarettes, 400 cigarillos, 200 cigars, 1kg tobacco, 20L aperitif, 90L wine (with a maximum amount of 60L sparkling wine) and 110L beer.

Travellers to the US who are residents of the country do not have to pay duty on

articles purchased overseas up to the value of $800, but there are limits on the amount of alcoholic beverages and to-

CURRENCY CONVERTER

£	€	€	£
1	1.14	1	0.88
3	3.43	3	2.63
5	5.70	5	4.38
13	14.85	13	11.38
40	46	40	35
75	86	75	66
120	137	120	105
250	286	250	219
500	571	500	438

$	€	€	$
1	0.81	1	1.23
3	2.43	3	3.70
5	4.05	5	6.17
13	10.54	13	16.04
40	32.42	40	49.35
75	61	75	92.52
120	97	120	148
250	203	250	308
500	405	500	617

For current exchange rates see www.xe.com

bacco products. For the regulations for international travel for US residents please see www.cbp.gov

DRINKING WATER

It is safe to drink the chlorinated tap water everywhere. Still mineral water (*metallikó neró*) is also available on ferries, in restaurants and cafés and is usually the same price as in the supermarkets.

DRIVING

For the entry with your own car, a national license and the motor vehicle registration should suffice; an international green insurance card is recommended. There is a good network of petrol stations on the islands. The use of seatbelts is compulsory for drivers and front passengers. The maximum speed in the towns is 50 km/h/30 mph, on national roads 90 km/h/56 mph. Maximum blood alcohol limit is 0.5 and 0.1 for motorcycle riders. Parking in a no parking zone is expensive: the fine costs 80 euros, most traffic violations are fined very heavily in Greece.

EARTHQUAKES

Light earthquakes do occur now and then and are no reason to panic. Should you experience an earthquake take cover underneath a door lintel, a table or a bed. As soon as the quake is over you should go outside (do not use the lifts) and then stay clear of walls and flower pots that might fall over. Once outside it's best to follow the lead of the locals.

ELECTRICITY

Greece has the same 220 volt as most continental European countries. You will need an adapter if you want to use a UK plug.

EMERGENCY SERVICES

Dial *112* for all the emergency services: police, fire brigade and ambulance. The number is toll free and English is also spoken.

ENTRANCE FEES

Pensioners over 65 from EU countries get reductions; children, young people and students from EU countries don't pay anything.

From November to March, entrance is free on Sundays for all visitors in museums and similar institutions. Other free entrance days are the first Sunday in April, May and October, the 6th of March, the last weekend in September, all international holidays as well as the International Remembrance Day in April, International Museum Day in May, World Environment Day in June and World Tourism Day in September.

FERRIES

Ferries sail from Killíni on the Peloponnese (which is quickly reached from Patras) to Zákynthos, to Póros/Kefaloniá and Pisoaétos/Ithaca. Year round connections are also operated between Nidrí/Léfkas, Fiskárdo/Kefaloniá and Fríkes/Ithaca. Ferries also sail from Ástakos on the mainland to Pisoaétos/Ithaca and Sámi/Kefaloniá. *www.ionionpelagos.com, www.kefalonianlines.com*

HEALTH

Well-trained doctors guarantee basic medical care on all major islands, however there is often a lack of technical equipment. If you are seriously ill, it is advisable to return home and this should be covered by your travel insurance.

You can be treated for free by doctors if you present the European Health Insurance Card issued by your own insurance company. However, in practice doctors do so reluctantly and it is better to pay cash, get a receipt and then present your bills to the insurance company for a refund.

There are pharmacies in the larger towns and villages; on the smaller islands, doctors have medication on hand for emergencies.

IMMIGRATION

A valid identity card or passport is sufficient. Children up to 12 years of age need a children's passport, children between 12 and 16 years can also travel with an ID card or a passport.

INFORMATION

GREEK NATIONAL TOURISM ORGANISATION (UK)
5th Floor East, Great Portland House | 4 Great Portland Street | London, W1W 8QJ | tel. 020 7495 9300 | www.visitgreece.gr

GREEK NATIONAL TOURISM ORGANISATION (USA)
800, Third Avenue, 23rd floor | New York, NY 10022 | tel. 212 421 5777 | www.visit greece.gr

INTERNET & WI-FI

Many hotels and cafés offer free WiFi to guests with their own laptop, iPhone or Smartphone. Internet terminals are available in some travel agencies at a fee. Internet cafés are used primarily for computer games by young locals.

LANGUAGE

The Greeks are proud of the characters in their language which are unique to Greece. Although place names and labels are often also written in Roman letters, it is still useful to have some knowledge of the Greek alphabet – and you really need to know how to stress the words

correctly to be understood. The vowel with the accent is always emphasised. The transcription of Greek names in the map section of this guide is based on the recommended international UN style. However, as this is seldom used on the islands, the text section of this guidebook is orientated on the standard pronunciation and spelling style used locally, although this also varies from town to town. It is sometimes the case that the same place name and its surroundings can have three to four different versions of spelling. A touch of imagination is required for finding your way around the island.

BUDGETING

Coffee	£2/$3.50
	for a cup of mocha
Taxi	£0.60/$0.95
	per kilometre
Wine	£2/$3.50
	for a glass of table wine
Gyros	£2/$3.50
	for a portion in pita bread
Petrol	£1.50/$2.50
	for 1 liter super
Deck chair	£3.50–£7/$5.50–£11
	for two with umbrella

MONEY & PRICES

The currency is the euro and you can withdraw money from many ATMs with your credit or debit card. Often your own bank will charge a fee, depending on the amount, making it cheaper to draw a large amount at once instead of a lot of small amounts. *Opening hours of the banks Mon–Thu 8am–2pm, Fri 8am–1.30pm.*

Price levels are more or less the same as elsewhere in Europe. Hotel rooms and public transport are cheaper, petrol and foodstuff more expensive.

NEWSPAPERS

English magazines and newspapers are available at most holiday resorts on the island within a day or two of publication. The weekly English *Athens News* is also published.

OPENING HOURS

Shops for the tourist trade are open daily 10am–10pm. Supermarkets are usually open from Monday to Saturday 8am–8pm. Many non-tourist shops are closed on Monday and Wednesday afternoons.

The majority of restaurants are open daily in high season; dance clubs usually only open at about 11pm or midnight. The opening hours specified in this travel guide are subject to frequent changes.

PHONE & MOBILE PHONE

With the exception of emergency numbers, all Greek phone numbers have ten digits. There is no area dialling code. Greek mobile phone numbers always begin with "6". Telephone booths with card telephones are very common in the towns, villages and on country roads. They are mainly operated by the telephone company OTE/COSMOTE which has offices in most cities. Telephone cards can be bought at kiosks and in supermarkets.

WEATHER ON ZÁKYNTHOS

	Jan	Feb	March	April	May	June	July	Aug	Sept	Oct	Nov	Dec
Daytime temperatures in °C/°F °	14/57	14/57	16/61	19/66	24/75	28/82	31/88	32/90	28/82	23/73	19/66	16/61
Nighttime temperatures in °C/°F	5/41	5/41	7/45	9/48	12/54	16/61	18/64	18/64	16/61	13/55	10/50	7/45
Sunshine hours/day	4	5	6	8	10	10	13	11	9	7	5	3
Precipitation days/month	13	11	9	7	5	2	1	1	5	9	12	15
Water temperatures in °C/°F	14/57	14/57	14/57	16/61	18/64	21/70	23/73	24/75	23/73	21/70	18/64	16/61

☀ Sunshine hours/day ➤ Precipitation days/month ≈≈≈ Water temperatures in °C/ °F

Mobile phone reception is good. When buying a Greek SIM card to obtain a Greek number, you will always have to present identification. SIM cards can be bought from 5 euros and are valid for a year after the last use. Mobile service providers are Cosmote, Vodafone and Wind.

The dialling code for Greece is +30. International dialling codes: UK +44, Australia +61, Canada +1, Ireland +353, and USA +1.

POST

There are post offices in all the towns and on almost all islands; they are mostly open from Monday to Friday 7am–3pm.

SMOKING

Smoking is prohibited in all enclosed public areas. However, outside of the towns and tourist centres the regulation is not taken seriously. The prices of cigarettes are slightly cheaper than elsewhere in Europe, and tobacco and cigarette paper for rolling your own cigarettes are common.

TAXI

Taxis are plentiful on all the islands. Only in the larger cities like Zákynthos Town are they equipped with taxi meters. In all the other cases the taxi (called *agoréon*) driver calculates the price according to the distance. A table showing distances and fares must be visible in every *agoréon*.

TIME

Greece is two hours ahead of Greenwich Mean Time, seven hours ahead of US Eastern Time and seven hours behind Australian Eastern Time.

TIPPING

10–15 per cent; tips below 50 cents are insulting. Chambermaids get 1 euro per room per day; in taxis you can round up the fare by at least 50 cents.

TOILETS

Apart from those in the hotels, Greek toilets my hold some surprises. Sometimes they are smart and fitted with modern Italian plumbing; others should be used only in emergencies. Even in good hotels, you are not allowed to flush the used toilet paper, but you have to put it in the bin provided. The reason is that it clogs up the narrow sewers and soakaways.

TOURS

Excursions by boat or bus are on offer in the larger holiday resorts and hotels, especially on Zákynthos. Bus tours normally take place with a local, government-licensed tour guide. The boat excursions on Zákynthos may also include a bus transfer from the hotel to the harbour and back.

WHEN TO GO

The Ionian Islands are suitable only in the summer months as a tourist destination. Since almost all of them depend very much on tourism, many shops, restaurants, and hotels that are not in the island capitals are closed from mid-October until April. During this time the islands can seem eerily empty, transport links are limited and the weather can also be very unpleasant due to storms and rainfall.

USEFUL PHRASES GREEK

PRONUNCIATION

We have provided a simple pronunciation aid for the Greek words
(see middle column). Note the following:
' the following syllable is emphasised
ð in Greek (shown as "dh" in middle column) is like "th" in "there"
θ in Greek (shown as "th" in middle column) is like "th" in "think"
Χ in Greek (shown as "ch" in middle column) is like a rough "h" or
"ch" in Scottish "loch"

Α	α	a	Η	η	i	Ν	ν	n	Τ	τ	t
Β	β	v	Θ	θ	th	Ξ	ξ	ks, x	Υ	υ	i, y
Γ	γ	g, y	Ι	ι	i, y	Ο	ο	o	Φ	φ	f
Δ	δ	th	Κ	κ	k	Π	π	p	Χ	χ	ch
Ε	ε	e	Λ	λ	l	Ρ	ρ	r	Ψ	ψ	ps
Ζ	ζ	z	Μ	μ	m	Σ	σ, ς s, ss			Ω	ώ	o

IN BRIEF

Yes/No/Maybe	ne/'ochi/'issos	Ναι/ Όχι/Ισως
Please/Thank you	paraka'lo/efcharis'to	Παρακαλώ/Ευχαριστώ
Sorry	sig'nomi	Συγνώμη
Excuse me	me sig'chorite	Με συγχωρείτε
May I...?	epi'treppete...?	Επιτρέπεται …?
Pardon?	o'riste?	Ορίστε?
I would like to.../	'thelo.../	Θέλω …/
have you got...?	'echete...?	Έχετε …?
How much is...?	'posso 'kani...?	Πόσο κάνει …?
I (don't) like this	Af'to (dhen) mu a'ressi	Αυτό (δεν) μου αρέσει
good/bad	ka'llo/kak'ko	καλό/κακό
too much/much/little	'para pol'li/pol'li/'ligo	πάρα πολύ/πολύ/λίγο
everything/nothing	ólla/'tipottal	όλα/τίποτα
Help!/Attention!/	vo'ithia!/prosso'chi!/	Βοήθεια!/Προσοχή!/
Caution!	prosso'chi!	Προσοχή!
ambulance	astheno'forro	Ασθενοφόρο
police/	astino'mia/	Αστυνομία/
fire brigade	pirosvesti'ki	Πυροσβεστική
ban/	apa'gorefsi/	Απαγόρευση/
forbidden	apago'revete	απαγορέυεται
danger/dangerous	'kindinoss/epi'kindinoss	Κίνδυνος/επικίνδυνος

Milás elliniká?

"Do you speak Greek?" This guide will help you to say the basic words and phrases in Greek

GREETINGS, FAREWELL

Good morning!/afternoon!/evening!/night!	kalli'mera/kalli'mera!/kalli'spera!/kalli'nichta!	Καλημέρα/Καλημέρα!/Καλησπέρα!/Καληνύχτα!
Hello!/goodbye!	'ya (su/sass)!/a'dio!/ya (su/sass)!	Γεία (σου/σας)!/αντίο!/Γεία (σου/σας)!
Bye!	me 'lene...	Με λένε …
My name is ...	poss sass 'lene?	Πως σας λένε?

DATE & TIME

Monday/Tuesday	dhef'tera/'triti	Δευτέρα/Τρίτη
Wednesday/Thursday	tet'tarti/'pempti	Τετάρτη/Πέμπτη
Friday/Saturday	paraske'vi/'savatto	Παρασκευή/Σάββατο
Sunday/weekday	kiria'ki/er'gassimi	Κυριακή/Εργάσιμη
today/tomorrow/yesterday	'simera/'avrio/chtess	Σήμερα/Αύριο/Χτες
What time is it?	ti 'ora 'ine?	Τι ώρα είναι?

TRAVEL

open/closed	annik'ta/klis'to	Ανοικτό/Κλειστό
entrance/	'issodhos/	Είσοδος/
driveway	'issodhos ochi'matonn	Είσοδος οχημάτων
exit	'eksodhos/	Έξοδος/
	'Eksodos ochi'matonn	Έξοδος οχημάτων
departure/	anna'chorissi/	Αναχώρηση/
departure/arrival	anna'chorissi/'afiksi	Αναχώρηση/Άφιξη
toilets/restrooms / ladies/	tual'lettes/gine'konn/	Τουαλέτες/Γυναικών/
gentlemen	an'dronn	Ανδρών
(no) drinking water	'possimo ne'ro	Πόσιμο νερό
Where is...?/Where are...?	pu 'ine...?/pu 'ine...?	Πού είναι/Πού είναι …?
bus/taxi	leofo'rio/tak'si	Λεωφορείο/Ταξί
street map/	'chartis tis 'pollis/	Χάρτης της πόλης/
map	'chartis	Χάρτης
harbour	li'mani	Λιμάνι
airport	a-ero'drommio	Αεροδρόμιο
schedule/ticket	drommo'logio/issi'tirio	Δρομολόγιο/Εισιτήριο
I would like to rent...	'thelo na nik'yasso...	Θέλω να νοικιάσω …
a car/a bicycle/	'enna afto'kinito/'enna	ένα αυτοκίνητο/ένα
a boat	po'dhilato/'mia 'varka	ποδήλατο/μία βάρκα
petrol/gas station	venzi'nadiko	Βενζινάδικο
petrol/gas / diesel	ven'zini/'diesel	Βενζίνη/Ντίζελ

FOOD & DRINK

Could you please book a table for tonight for four?	Klis'te mass parakal'lo 'enna tra'pezi ya a'popse ya 'tessera 'atoma	Κλείστε μας παρακαλώ ένα τραπέζι γιά απόψε γιά τέσσερα άτομα
The menu, please	tonn ka'taloggo parakal'lo	Τον κατάλογο παρακαλώ
Could I please have...?	tha 'ithella na 'echo...?	Θα ήθελα να έχο ...?
with/without ice/ sparkling	me/cho'ris 'pago/ anthrakik'ko	με/χωρίς πάγο/ ανθρακικό
vegetarian/allergy	chorto'fagos/allerg'ia	Χορτοφάγος/Αλλεργία
May I have the bill, please?	'thel'lo na pli'rosso parakal'lo	Θέλω να πληρώσω παρακαλώ

SHOPPING

Where can I find...?	pu tha vro...?	Που θα βρω ...?
pharmacy/ chemist	farma'kio/ ka'tastima	Φαρμακείο/Κατάστημα καλλυντικών
bakery/market	'furnos/ago'ra	Φούρνος/Αγορά
grocery	pandopo'lio	Παντοπωλείο
kiosk	pe'riptero	Περίπτερο
expensive/cheap/price	akri'vos/fti'nos/ti'mi	ακριβός/φτηνός/Τιμή
more/less	pio/li'gotere	πιό/λιγότερο

ACCOMMODATION

I have booked a room	'kratissa 'enna do'matio	Κράτησα ένα δωμάτιο
Do you have any... left?	'echete a'komma...	Έχετε ακόμα ...
single room	mon'noklino	Μονόκλινο
double room	'diklino	Δίκλινο
key	kli'dhi	Κλειδί
room card	ilektronni'ko kli'dhi	Ηλεκτρονικό κλειδί

HEALTH

doctor/dentist/ paediatrician	ya'tros/odhondoya'tros/ pe'dhiatros	Ιατρός/Οδοντογιατρός/ Παιδίατρος
hospital/ emergency clinic	nossoko'mio/ yatri'ko 'kentro	Νοσοκομείο/ Ιατρικό κέντρο
fever/pain	piret'tos/'ponnos	Πυρετός/Πόνος
diarrhoea/nausea	dhi'arria/ana'gula	Διάρροια/Αναγούλα
sunburn	ilia'ko 'engavma	Ηλιακό έγκαυμα
inflamed/ injured	molli'menno/ pligo'menno	μολυμένο /πληγωμένο
pain reliever/tablet	paf'siponna/'chapi	Παυσίπονο/Χάπι

POST, TELECOMMUNICATIONS & MEDIA

stamp/letter	gramma'tossimo/'gramma	Γραμματόσημο/Γράμμα
postcard	kartpos'tall	Καρτ-ποστάλ
I need a landline phone card	kri'azomme 'mia tile'karta ya dhi'mossio tilefoni'ko 'thalamo	Χρειάζομαι μία τηλεκάρτα για δημόσιο τηλεφωνικό θάλαμο
I'm looking for a prepaid card for my mobile	tha 'ithella 'mia 'karta ya to kinni'to mu	Θα ήθελα μία κάρτα για το κινητό μου
Where can I find internet access?	pu bor'ro na vro 'prosvassi sto índernett?	Που μπορώ να βρω πρόσβαση στο ίντερνετ;
socket/adapter/charger	'briza/an'dapporras/fortis'tis	πρίζα/αντάπτορας/φορτιστής
computer/battery/rechargeable battery	ippologis'tis/batta'ria/eppanaforti'zomenni batta'ria	Υπολογιστής/μπαταρία/επαναφορτιζόμενη μπαταρία
internet connection/wifi	'sindhessi se as'sirmato 'dhitio/vaifai	Σύνδεση σε ασύρματο δίκτυο/WiFi

LEISURE, SPORTS & BEACH

beach	para'lia	Παραλία
sunshade/lounger	om'brella/ksap'plostra	Ομπρέλα/Ξαπλώστρα

NUMBERS

0	mi'dhen	μηδέν
1	'enna	ένα
2	'dhio	δύο
3	'tria	τρία
4	'tessera	τέσσερα
5	'pende	πέντε
6	'eksi	έξι
7	ef'ta	εφτά
8	och'to	οχτώ
9	e'nea	εννέα
10	'dhekka	δέκα
11	'endhekka	ένδεκα
12	'dodhekka	δώδεκα
20	'ikossi	είκοσι
50	pen'inda	πενήντα
100	eka'to	εκατό
200	dhia'kossia	διακόσια
1000	'chilia	χίλια
10000	'dhekka chil'iades	δέκα χιλιάδες

ROAD ATLAS

■■■ The green line indicates the Discovery Tour "Ionian islands at a glance"
■■■ The blue line indicates the other Discovery Tours

All tours are also marked on the pull-out map

Photo: View of the bay, Kióni, Ithaca

Exploring the Ionian Islands

The map on the back cover shows how the area has been sub-divided

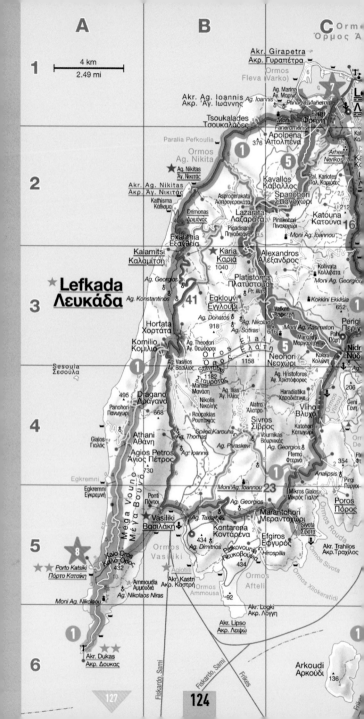

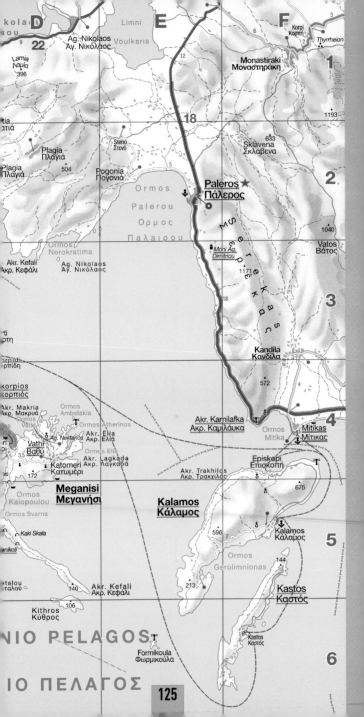

kola **D**
ou

Limni **E**

F Korpi
Κόρπη

Thyrrheion

22 Ag. Nikolaos
Αγ. Νικόλαος

Voulkaria

1

Monastiraki
Μοναστηράκη

Lamía
Λαμία
396

12

1193

18

Steno
Στενό

Sklavena
Σκλάβενα

633

tia
τιά

Plagia –
Πλαγιά

504

2

Plagia
Πλαγιά

Pogonia
Πογονιά

5

Paleros ★
Πάλερος

1040

O r m o s

P a l e r o u

Ο ρ μ ο ς

Π α λ α ι ρ ο υ

Vatos
Βάτος

Ormos
Nerokratima

Moni Ag.
Dimitriou

Akr. Kefali
Ακρ. Κεφάλι

Ag. Nikolaos
Αγ. Νικόλαος

1171

18

3

ti
ρη

πρίδη
ρπίδη

Kandila
Κανδίλα

korpios
κορπιός

572

4

Akr. Makria
Ακρ. Μακρυά

Ormos
Ambelakia

Akr. Kamilafka
Ακρ. Καμιλάυκα

Mitikas ★
Μίτικας

4

us

Ormos
Vatsa

Ormos
Atherinos

Akr. Elia
Ακρ. Ελιά

Ormos
Mitika

ri
Vathi
Βαθύ

Ag. Nektarios

Akr. Lagkada
Ακρ. Λαγκάδα

Episkopi
Επισκοπή

3.5

172

Katomeri
Κατωμέρι

Akr. Trakhilos
Ακρ. Τράκχιλος

675

Meganisi
Μεγανήσι

Ormos
Kalopoulou

Kalamos
Κάλαμος

Ormos Svarna

5

Kaki Skala

596

7

Kalamos
Κάλαμος

anikoli

Ormos
Gerolimnionas

144

etalou
αταλού

140

Akr. Kefali
Ακρ. Κεφάλι

213

Kastos
Καστός

106

Kithros
Κύθρος

6

NIO PELAGOS

Kastos
Καστός

Formikoula
Φωρμικούλα

Grid labels

A **B** **C**

1 4 km
2.49 mi

2

I O N I O   P E L A G O S

I O N I O   Π Ε Λ Α Γ Ο Σ

3

4

5

6

Map labels

Akr. Dafnoudi
Ακρ. Δαφνούδη

Antipa
Αντιπάρ

Manga
Μάγγ

Tzamarella
Τζαμαρέλλα

Drap
Δραπ

Ormos Asso

★★ Frourio Assou

Asso
Άσσο

2

Akr. Atheras
Ακρ. Αθέρας

Ormos Athera

Akr. Kakata
Ακρ. Κακατά

Akr. Asprokavos
Ακρ. Ασπρόχαβος

Ormos Mirtos ★★ Ormos Mirtou

Akr. Ag. Kiriaki
Ακρ. Αγ. Κυριακή

221

350

Ag. Spirido
Αγ. Σπιρίδω

Akr. Ag. Ioannis
Ακρ. Αγ. Ιωάννης

Ormos
Ag. Kiriakis

Drak
Δρακ

518

Ag. Ioannis

Atheras
Αθέρας

Zola
Ζώλα

455

Agkonas
Αγγώνας

4

Nifi
Νύφη

806

250

Petrikata
Πετρικάτα

Riza
Ρήζα

Kardakata
Καρδακάτα

924

188

Ormos Pethani
Ακρ. Ortholithia
Ακρ. Όρθολιθία

Ormos

Ormos
Livadi
Λιβάδι

Kontogourata
Κοντογούρατα

Vonikes
Βονίκες

Vilatoria
Βιλατώρια

Kontogenada
Κοντογενάδα

Argostoliou

Kourouklata
Κουρουκλάτα

943

Enmorfia
Ευμορφία

1043

Ag. Thekli
Αγ. Θέκλη

Skineas 180
Σκινέας

Kouvalata
Κουβαλάτα

Dilinata
Διλινάτα

Damoulianata
Δαμουλιάνατα

Parisata
Παρισάτα

18

Monopolata
Μονοπόλατα

Ag. Dimitrios
Αγ. Δημήτριος

Moni
Kehrionos

Ormos

Farsa
Φάρσα

Dafgata
Δαφγάτα

Kaminarata
Καμινάρατα

Mantoukata
Μαντουκάτα

Argostoliou

2

84

Kipouria
Κηπούρια

Moni Ag.
Paraskevi Tafiou

Favata
Φαβατά

Katerelata
Κατερελάτα

Lixouri
Λιξούρι

Farak
Φαρα

Havdata
Χαβδάτα

Tipaldata
Τιπάλδατα

6

Katavothres
Καταβόθρες

50

Moni Y. Th.
Kipourion

186

Soullari
Σούλλαρη

1

Mihalitsata
Μιχαλιτσάτα

Lepeda
Λέπεδα

Argostoli
Αργοστόλ

Raza
Ραζα

Havriata
Χαβριάτα

Lagkadakia
Λαγκαδάκια

Mantzavinata
Μαντζα-
βινάτα

Vouni
Βούνι

78

Viata
Βιάτα

126

Moni Prof. Ilia

Akr. Skinos
Ακρ. Σκίνος

128

Ag. Nikolaos
Αγ. Νικόλαος

Lassi
Λάσση

Krani

Ormos Vatsa

Kilini

Spilia
Σπηλιά

Moni
Pan

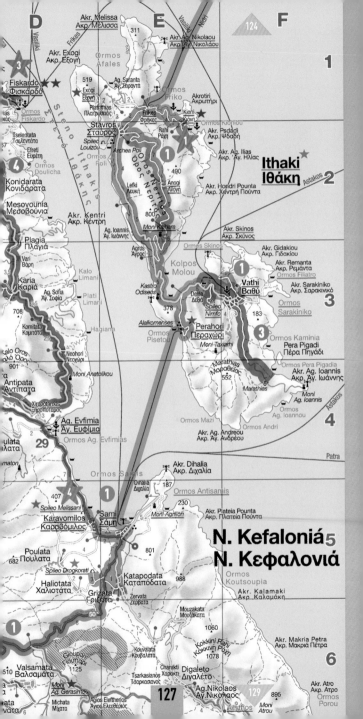

Akr. Ortholithia
Ακρ. Ορθολίθια
Vonikes
Βονικές
Vilatoria
Βιλατόρια
Ag. Thekli
Άγ. Θέκλη

A

Livadi
Λιβάδι

Ormos
Argostoliou

B

943

C

Kourouklata
Κουρουκλάτα

Enmorfia
Ευμορφία
1043

Kontogenada
Κοντογενάδα
Skineas
Σκινέας   180

Kouvalata
Κουβαλάτα

Dilinata
Διλινάτα

1 Damoulianata
Δαμουλιανάτα

Parisata
Παρισάτα

Monopolata
Μονοπολάτα

Ag. Dimitrios
Αγ. Δημήτριος
Moni
Kehrionos

Ormos
Ορμός
Argostoliou
Αργοστολίου

Farsa
Φάρσα

Dafgata
Δαφγάτα

1000

Kaminarata
Καμινάρατα

Mantoukata
Μαντουκάτα

Favata
Φαβάτα

Moni Ag.
Paraskevi Taflou

Katerelata
Κατερελάτα

Lixouri
Λιξούρη

Faraklata
Φαράκλατα

846

Havdata
Χαβδάτα

Tipaldata
Τιπάλδατα

Katavothres
Καταβόθρες

Argostoli
Αργοστόλι

673

24

Havriata
Χαβριάτα

Mihalitsata
Μιχαλιτσάτα

Razata
Ραζάτα

50

2 Lagkadakia
Λαγκαδάκια
Akr. Skinos
Ακρ. Σκίνος

Vouni
Βουνί

Ag. Nikolaos
Άγ. Νικόλαος   78

Mantzavinata
Μαντζαβινάτα

Lepeda
Λεπέδα

Lassi
Λάσση

Moni Prof. Ilias

Fragkata
Φραγκάτα

Ormos
Vatsa

Xi
Ξι

Mega Lakos
Μέγα Λάκος

Akr. Ag. Georgios
Ακρ. Αγ. Γεώργιος

Spilia
Σπήλια

Ag. Gerassimou

Moni Ag.
Paraskevis

Troia
Τροία

Makris Gialos
Μακρής Γιαλός

9

Krani

Demoutsanata
Δεμουτσανάτα

Mita
Μήτ

Makris Gialos

Kokolata
Κοκολάτα

Kokolata
Κοκολάτα

Ag. Georgiou

Kastro
Κάστρο

Pera
Περ

Akrotiri
Kounopetra
Κουνόπετρα

Vardiani
Βαρδιάνι

Kompothekrata
Κομποθέκρατα

Platis Gialos

242

Menegata
Μενεγάτα

Metaxata
Μεταξάτα

Moni
Milapi

Ken
Κε

3

Ormos Vatsa

Aerolimenas
Kefallonia

Minia
Μίνια

Lakithra
Λακήθρα

Dorota
Δώρατα

Spi
Σπ

Klismata
Κλήσματα
Kaligata
Καλλιγάτα

Akr. Ag. Nikolaou
Ακρ. Άγ. Νικολάου

Svoronata
Σβορωνάτα

Ormos Ammes

Ammes
Άμμες

Koriana
Κοριάνα

Akr. Ag. Pelagia
Ακρ. Άγ. Πελαγία

Ormos
Avithos

110

1

Thionisi
Θυονήσι

4

5

I O N I O

I O N I O

6

4 km
2.49 mi

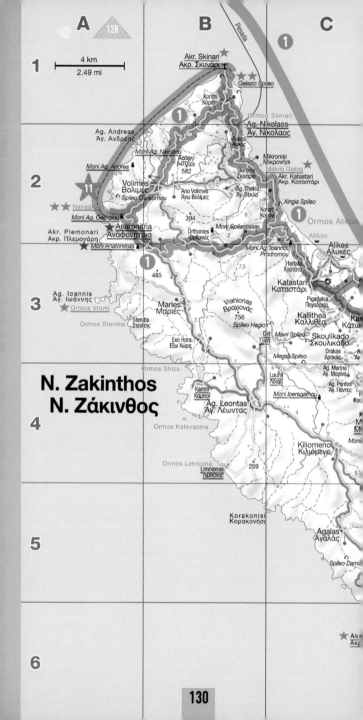

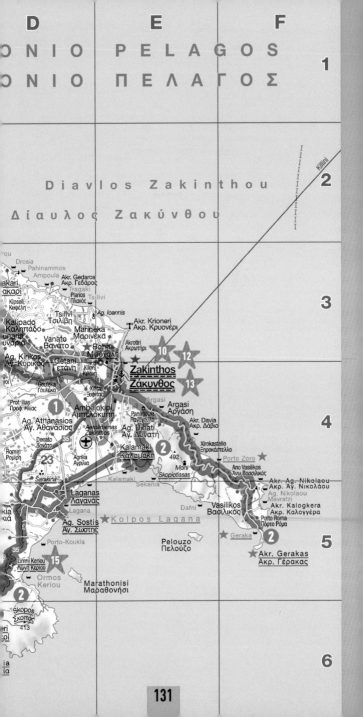

KEY TO ROAD ATLAS

Autobahn · Gebührenpflichtige Anschlussstelle · Gebührenstelle · Anschlussstelle mit Nummer · Rasthaus mit Übernachtung · Raststätte · Kleinraststätte · Tankstelle · Parkplatz mit und ohne WC		Motorway · Toll junction · Toll station · Junction with number · Motel · Restaurant · Snackbar · Filling-station · Parking place with and without WC
Autobahn in Bau und geplant mit Datum der voraussichtlichen Verkehrsübergabe		Motorway under construction and projected with expected date of opening
Zweibahnige Straße (4-spurig)		Dual carriageway (4 lanes)
Fernverkehrsstraße · Straßennummern		Trunk road · Road numbers
Wichtige Hauptstraße		Important main road
Hauptstraße · Tunnel · Brücke		Main road · Tunnel · Bridge
Nebenstraßen		Minor roads
Fahrweg · Fußweg		Track · Footpath
Wanderweg (Auswahl)		Tourist footpath (selection)
Eisenbahn mit Fernverkehr		Main line railway
Zahnradbahn, Standseilbahn		Rack-railway, funicular
Kabinenschwebebahn · Sessellift		Aerial cableway · Chair-lift
Autofähre · Personenfähre		Car ferry · Passenger ferry
Schifffahrtslinie		Shipping route
Naturschutzgebiet · Sperrgebiet		Nature reserve · Prohibited area
Nationalpark · Naturpark · Wald		National park · natural park · Forest
Straße für Kfz. gesperrt		Road closed to motor vehicles
Straße mit Gebühr		Toll road
Straße mit Wintersperre		Road closed in winter
Straße für Wohnanhänger gesperrt bzw. nicht empfehlenswert		Road closed or not recommended for caravans
Touristenstraße · Pass		Tourist route · Pass
Schöner Ausblick · Rundblick · Landschaftlich bes. schöne Strecke		Scenic view · Panoramic view · Route with beautiful scenery
Heilbad · Schwimmbad		Spa · Swimming pool
Jugendherberge · Campingplatz		Youth hostel · Camping site
Golfplatz · Sprungschanze		Golf-course · Ski jump
Kirche im Ort, freistehend · Kapelle		Church · Chapel
Kloster · Klosterruine		Monastery · Monastery ruin
Synagoge · Moschee		Synagogue · Mosque
Schloss, Burg · Schloss-, Burgruine		Palace, castle · Ruin
Turm · Funk-, Fernsehturm		Tower · Radio-, TV-tower
Leuchtturm · Kraftwerk		Lighthouse · Power station
Wasserfall · Schleuse		Waterfall · Lock
Bauwerk · Marktplatz, Areal		Important building · Market place, area
Ausgrabungs- u. Ruinenstätte · Bergwerk		Arch. excavation, ruins · Mine
Dolmen · Menhir · Nuraghen		Dolmen · Menhir · Nuraghe
Hünen-, Hügelgrab · Soldatenfriedhof		Cairn · Military cemetery
Hotel, Gasthaus, Berghütte · Höhle		Hotel, inn, refuge · Cave

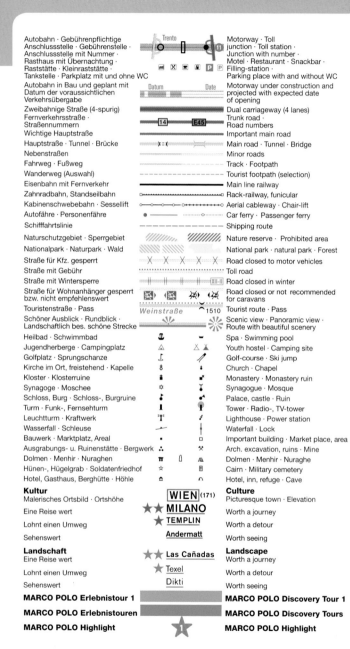

Kultur		**Culture**
Malerisches Ortsbild · Ortshöhe	**WIEN** (171)	Picturesque town · Elevation
Eine Reise wert	★★ **MILANO**	Worth a journey
Lohnt einen Umweg	★ **TEMPLIN**	Worth a detour
Sehenswert	<u>Andermatt</u>	Worth seeing
Landschaft		**Landscape**
Eine Reise wert	★★ **Las Cañadas**	Worth a journey
Lohnt einen Umweg	★ **Texel**	Worth a detour
Sehenswert	<u>Dikti</u>	Worth seeing
MARCO POLO Erlebnistour 1		**MARCO POLO Discovery Tour 1**
MARCO POLO Erlebnistouren		**MARCO POLO Discovery Tours**
MARCO POLO Highlight	★	**MARCO POLO Highlight**

FOR YOUR NEXT TRIP...

MARCO POLO TRAVEL GUIDES

Travel with
Insider
Tips

INDEX

This index lists all islands, places and destinations featured in this guide. Numbers in bold indicate a main entry.

CREDITS

WRITE TO US

-mail: info@marcopologuides.co.uk

id you have a great holiday?
s there something on your mind?
Whatever it is, let us know!
Whether you want to praise, alert us
o errors or give us a personal tip –
MARCO POLO would be pleased to
ear from you.
We do everything we can to provide the
ery latest information for your trip.

Nevertheless, despite all of our authors'
thorough research, errors can creep in.
MARCO POLO does not accept any
liability for this. Please contact us by
e-mail or post.

MARCO POLO Travel Publishing Ltd
Pinewood, Chineham Business Park
Crockford Lane, Chineham Basingstoke,
Hampshire RG24 8AL
United Kingdom

PICTURE CREDITS
Cover photograph: Shipwreck Beach, Zákynthos (Laif: T. u. B. Morandi)
Photographs: Diving Center Turtle Beach: J. Schierholz/K. Pöllny (18 bottom); Gettyimages/Staff: S. Gallup (99);
Gettyimages: D. Boskovic (59), M. P. Chapman (19 bottom), M. Colombo (2), R. Dan (104/105), A. Nakic (3), B. Trdina
(44/45), Gettyimages/Heritage Images/Kontributor (24/25); Gettyimages/robertharding: F. Fell (11); J. Gibson (18 top);
Glow Images: Harding (5, 100/101); Glow Images/EWAStock (107); R. Hackenberg (9, 10, 14/15); huber-images: O.
Fantuz (81); huber-images/SIME: M. Ripani (6); Laif: T. u. B. Morandi (1); Laif/Le Figaro Magazine (37, 38/39, 111); Laif/
Robert Harding Productions/robertharding (63, 110 top, 122/123); Laif/robertharding: S. Black (12/13), F. Fell (75, 76);
Look/age fotostock (54, 79); Look/Blend Images (60); Look/robertharding (40); Look/TerraVista (42); mauritius im-
ages: S. Beuthan (31), M. Habel (20/21, 30, 66, 84/85); mauritius images/age fotostock: J. Wlodarczyk (64/65); mauritius images/Alamy: P. Atkinson (68), G. Atsametakis (17), I. G. Dagnall (flap left), S. French (52/53), G. Gajewski (46),
T. Harris (109), C. Iliopoulos (4 top,32/33, 49, 94), D. Kilpatrick (72), J. Lackie (18 centre), M. Longhurst (89), H. Milas
(56), J. Morgan 08 (108), M. Pizzocaro (50), R. Wyatt (29), C. Rout (7), D. Tomlinson (34); mauritius images/foodcol-
lection (4 bottom, 26/27, 71); mauritius images/funkyfood London/Alamy: P. Williams (23); mauritius images/gbim-
ages/Alamy (8); mauritius images/Hemis.fr: B. Gardel (82); mauritius images/ib/gourmet-vision (28 right); mauritius
images/imagebroker: Eisele-Hein (28 left); mauritius images/Juice Images: I. Lishman (96, 102); mauritius images/
Westend61/zerocreatives (19 top); mauritius images/Zoonar/Alamy (flap right); Naundorf/Siegmann (110 bottom)

2nd edition – fully revised and updated 2019
Worldwide Distribution: Marco Polo Travel Publishing Ltd, Pinewood, Chineham Business Park,
Crockford Lane, Basingstoke, Hampshire RG24 8AL, United Kingdom. E-mail: sales@marcopolouk.com
© MAIRDUMONT GmbH & Co. KG, Ostfildern
Chief editor: Stefanie Penck
Author: Klaus Bötig; editor: Nadia Al Kureischi, Arnd M. Schuppius
Programme supervision: Lucas Forst-Gill, Susanne Heimburger, Johanna Jiranek, Nikolai Michaelis, Kristin
Wittemann, Tim Wohlbold; Picture editors: Gabriele Forst, Stefanie Wiese
Cartography road atlas: © MAIRDUMONT, Ostfildern; Cartography pull-out map: © MAIRDUMONT, Ostfildern
Design front cover, p. 1, pull-out map cover: Karl Anders – Büro für Visual Stories, Hamburg; interior: milchhof:atelier,
Berlin; Discovery Tours, p. 2/3: Susan Chaaban Dipl.-Des. (FH)
Translated from German by Wendy Barrows, Susan Jones; Prepress: writehouse, Cologne
Phrase book in cooperation with Ernst Klett Sprachen GmbH, Stuttgart,
Editorial by Pons Wörterbücher

MIX
Paper from
responsible sources
FSC® C124385

DOS & DON'TS ✋

There are few tourist traps. But you should look out for some things

DON'T PHOTOGRAPH WITHOUT PERMISSION

Many Greeks love to have their photograph taken, but dislike tourists that act as though they are on safari. Before you just start snapping away, smile at the person you want to photograph and wait for their permission.

DON'T BE FLEECED

If you feel you have been overpriced in a shop or restaurant, always ask for a bill or receipt for the purchased items or service and if necessary, threaten to go to the tourist police. If the shop or restaurant owner has a bad conscience, he will not want the matter to be taken further.

DON'T BE SHOCKED BY THE PRICE OF FISH

In restaurants and tavernas, fresh fish is very expensive and is often sold by weight. Always ask for the kilo price first and when the fish is being weighed, make sure you are present to avoid any unpleasant surprises.

DON'T HIKE IN SANDALS

Sandals are not even suitable for short hikes; at least wear sturdy trainers. The paths are often stony and slippery. And there are (venomous) snakes – only a few and they are timid – but it is best to be cautious. Long trousers will protect you from thorns.

DO COVER UP IN CHURCH

Greeks are used to seeing some skin in the beach resorts but in the villages you should dress more conservatively. In the churches and monasteries it is expected that knees and shoulders be covered.

DON'T ASK ABOUT THE COMPETITION

Greeks are very honest. But don't go into a taverna and ask about another one! You will be told that it doesn't exist, that the owner has passed away or that the police have closed it down.

DON'T TAKE ANTIQUES

Antiques, old weavings and embroidery as well as old icons may only be exported with special permission. Taking stones from an archaeological site or even digging yourself is an offence liable for prosecution.

DON'T TRUST "HANDMADE"

The icons in the souvenir shops are often described as "handmade". But it is usually only a silkscreen print done by hand and not a genuinely handmade icon.

DON'T LEAVE THE ASPHALT

If you are travelling with a hired vehicle and leave the road, you will be driving without insurance and will have to pay for any damages yourself. Tyre damage is not insured even if the damage occurred on a surfaced road.